Computer Languages:
A Practical Guide to the Chief
Programming Languages

Computer Languages:
A Practical Guide to the Chief Programming Languages

PETER C. SANDERSON, M.A.

Senior Lecturer in Computing,
Wandsworth Technical College, London

LONDON
NEWNES-BUTTERWORTHS

ENGLAND: BUTTERWORTH & CO. (PUBLISHERS) LTD.
                LONDON: 88 Kingsway, W.C.2.
AUSTRALIA: BUTTERWORTH & CO. (AUSTRALIA) LTD.
                SYDNEY: 20 Loftus Street
                MELBOURNE: 343 Little Collins Street
                BRISBANE: 240 Queen Street
CANADA: BUTTERWORTH & CO. (CANADA) LTD.
                TORONTO: 14 Curity Avenue, 374
NEW ZEALAND: BUTTERWORTH & CO. (NEW ZEALAND) LTD.
                WELLINGTON: 49/51 Ballance Street
                AUCKLAND: 35 High Street
SOUTH AFRICA: BUTTERWORTH & CO. (SOUTH AFRICA) LTD.
                DURBAN: 33/35 Beach Grove

First published 1970

72-4529

Printed in Great Britain by John Wright & Sons Ltd., Bristol

CONTENTS

PREFACE

The rapid increase of the use of computers in business, scientific research, engineering and education has led to a wide interest in computer programming.

This book is believed to be the only work on the market providing an introduction to *all* the chief high-level computer languages in common use. It is intended to be useful to programmers who wish to acquire the essentials of an unfamiliar computer language, as well as to beginners who wish to have a knowledge of more than one computer language. Installations differ in the languages used, so that it is an essential widening of a programmer's experience to learn more than one high-level computer language.

No knowledge of higher mathematics is required for the comprehension of this work, and it will assist sixth formers, undergraduates and research students, who are making their first acquaintance with computer programming, to feel at ease with standard computer languages. The materials, examples and problems in chapters 4–8 have been used in the past four years for a variety of courses for research workers, accountants, engineers, doctors, undergraduates and sixth formers.

Chapters 1–3 are introductory and discuss briefly the basic components of a digital computer, the general planning of a computer program without regard to a particular language, and the various types of computer language.

The rest of the book discusses the basic features of the most useful high-level computer languages in some detail with an emphasis on those features that can be used on more than one type of computer. These chapters are self-contained so that there is no necessity to read them consecutively. It must be emphasized that the programming manual for an individual computer should be consulted for the variations which exist for some computer languages and that practice alone makes a competent programmer. To get full benefit from this book, the reader should have access to a computer.

I must acknowledge in particular Mr. E. A. Price of Ealing Technical College, Mr. R. C. Turner and Mr. H. Howells of Wandsworth Technical College, and Mr. D. Hendry of the University of London Institute of Computer Science for helpful suggestions about the book; Mr. C. F. Schofield of the University of London Institute of Computer Science for placing at my disposal his researches into Fortran dialects; Mr. W. Naney IBM(UK) Development Laboratories Ltd. and Mr. A. Borland of IBM(UK) Ltd. for many useful suggestions for chapter 7; Mr. B. Wiggins of IBM(UK) Ltd. for assistance with the testing of PL/I programs; the staff of ICSL at Newman Street for assistance in punching and testing the suggested solutions to chapters 4, 5 and 8; ICL for valuable advice on chapter 8 and for permission to reproduce Fig. 3 and to mention features of EMA and details of Atlas Algol; Mr. A. R. Kench and Mr. O. Vellacott of GEIS Ltd. for assistance with the appendix; Corinne Smither and Gillian Towers for producing a typescript from hieroglyphics, and the staff of the publishers for their helpfulness and guidance.

P. C. S.

INTRODUCTION TO DIGITAL COMPUTERS

The debates of the House of Lords perhaps command less attention than they deserve, especially on the eve of a general election. It is hardly surprising, therefore, that the quotation below failed to have its significance adequately appreciated.

"We are stepping into a real revolution which for want of a better name I may call the Cybernetic Revolution. It will alter most working lives more than the industrial revolution ever did . . . . The computer which is part, though only part, of this cybernetic revolution is the most wonderful machine invented by man. It is a deep and mysterious machine; very much more than a mere calculating machine."†

Computers are having a greater and greater impact on our daily lives. Bills, bank statements and investment accounts are usually now produced by a computer, which is an ideal machine for routine accounting procedures because of its fantastic speed and accuracy. Yet, as Lord Snow so aptly remarked, the computer must not be considered as just another office accounting machine. The versatility of the computer is shown by the numerous different tasks it performs. Computers are used to guide satellites, control machine tools, prepare literary concordances and forecast the weather. More unusual uses of computers include the preparation of saleable abstract art and the composition of music. The complexity of their electronic construction produces a feeling of baffled wonderment in the layman. However, it is not necessary to understand the inner workings of a computer in order to utilize its potential. Many programmers have little, if any, familiarity with the constructional details of the computer.

Basically there are two kinds of computer; the analogue computer and the digital computer. This book is concerned with the programming of digital computers, and in the ensuing chapters the word *computer* will always refer to the digital computer.

A computer can be defined as an electronic machine for the manipulation of symbols in a predetermined manner without the intervention of an operator. In most cases the symbol manipulation is numerical, but computers are also used for such non-numerical applications as the

† Lord Snow, House of Lords, 2 March 1966 (*Hansard*, pp. 702–3).

automatic translation of languages. The electronic digital computer is a general-purpose machine, so that the same computer can be used for producing invoices, solving differential equations or textually analysing a document. Since the computer is an electronic machine, the computational speeds defy imagination. A typical modern computer is capable of adding two numbers in six microseconds. A microsecond is a millionth of a second and has approximately the same relationship to a second as a second has to twelve days!

These high speeds would be of mere academic interest if a computer was operated by manual keyboard operation like the conventional adding machine. The sequence of instructions for a computer to obey is known as a *program*. This program is stored inside the computer which then proceeds to obey the instructions in the desired sequence without need for continual operator intervention. The ability to store its own instructions is the vital distinction between the computer and other calculating devices, and some of the earliest computers were known as *stored program calculators*.

A typical series of steps when using a computer to perform calculations could be:

1. Punch the instructions in paper tape (or punched cards), insert the tape in the reader attached to the computer and press the *start* button so that the instructions are stored inside the computer.
2. Punch the data on which the program has to perform the desired calculations into cards or tape and insert the data in the reader.
3. Press the *start* button; the calculations are then performed on the data and the results printed out without the need for further operator intervention.

The computer always obeys the program exactly, and sometimes has been given the soubriquet of the "thoroughly obedient moron". If a programmer omits vital instructions, the computer cannot be expected to have telepathic insight into his intentions; even the *stop* instruction at the end of a program must be supplied.

The computer will attempt to obey nonsensical instructions such as division by zero and the extraction of a square root of a negative number. The action taken here varies considerably from one computer to another.

Certain basic components are common to all computers from the small desk-top machines to the gigantic computers, which are capable of running several programs simultaneously. Before these components are reviewed, it will be considered how a human operator would perform a computation using a desk calculator.

The operator has a list of instructions as to how the computation is to be performed, a 'scratch-pad' to record intermediate results, initial data consisting of the numbers on which the computation is to be performed, and paper on which to write the final results. The similar components of a simple electronic computing system are shown in Fig. 1.

The computer *store* contains the instructions and intermediate results; the *input units* read the data under the control of the program; the *output units* print or display the answer, and the arithmetic unit contains the circuitry to perform the desired calculations. The *control unit* can be compared to the brain of the operator of the calculating machine. It initiates commands to the appropriate circuitry as required by the program instructions. More details will now be given about these components.

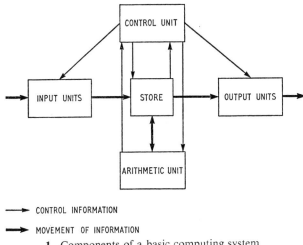

⟶ CONTROL INFORMATION

➡ MOVEMENT OF INFORMATION

1. Components of a basic computing system

Input devices

The most common methods of presenting information to a computer are the use of punched paper tape or punched cards. Since these inevitably involve transcription of the data for punching, other methods have been developed of presenting information to a computer in a form which is readable to man. One example of this can be found in the 'hieroglyphics' at the bottom of cheques (code E13B), which can be read by a special reader attached to a computer and also (with a little imagination) by human readers.

Punched paper tape

Information can be represented on a continuous strip of paper tape by punching round holes across the tape (Fig. 2). Each character has a unique pattern of holes. The tape is usually produced by a special typewriter that punches a pattern of holes for each character typed and for various carriage controls such as space and carriage return.

There are many paper-tape codes using from five to eight positions (sometimes referred to as channels or tracks) across the tape. There is a standard tape code known as the ISO code but some computers do not use it. The paper-tape reader attached to a modern computer senses the pattern of holes photoelectrically and puts the character in the store of the computer. A reader can commonly read 1000 characters a second.

1234567890

2. Punched paper tape

Punched cards

The most usual form of punched card read by a computer is shown in Fig. 3. This card is divided into 80 columns, each of which has 12 punching positions. One, two or three oblong holes can be punched in any column to represent a number, a letter or a special symbol (often a punctuation mark). The printing on the face of the card varies; the illustration shows a standard card. The method of representing letters and numbers on 80-column cards is universal, but there are differences in the representation of other characters.

3. Typical punched card

Punched cards are usually prepared with a key-punch or a typewriter attached to a key-punch. Most computers read the cards photoelectrically. Usual reading speeds are between 600 and 1000 cards a minute. There is a highly sophisticated range of machinery for punched-card data processing. Possession of such machines as punched-card sorters is often a factor in the choice of punched cards as the preferred input medium for the computer.

There have been exhaustive discussions as to the relative merits of cards and paper tape as computer input media, and it is not proposed to initiate another one here. Considerations relevant to a particular firm or organization usually determine the choice.

The typewriter

The majority of computers have a typewriter that is directly connected to the computer store and that can be used for the insertion of instructions and data. Its chief use is for insertion of information by a skilled computer operator and for the transmission of queries when a rapid response is required.

Output devices

The line printer

The most useful output device for most purposes is the line printer; this prints a line at a time, unlike a teleprinter which prints only a single character at a time. A common number of characters in a line is 120.

The main types of line printer are known as the *chain printer* and *barrel printer*. On the chain printer, characters are embossed on the outer edge of a metal chain that revolves continuously past the paper. On a barrel printer, the characters appear in each print position around the circumference of a solid metal barrel. When the desired character passes the appropriate print position, a hammer presses the paper against a carbon ribbon separating the paper and the characters. In spite of the rotation of the chain or barrel, the high speed of the hammers produces clear and definite printing.

Printing is done on continuous stationery that is guided through the printer by sprocket holes at the edge of the paper. Semi-perforated divisions divide the continuous roll of paper into sheets. Average printing speeds are between 600 and 1000 lines a minute.

Typical line-printer output can be seen in the majority of gas, electricity and telephone bills.

Punched output

Punched paper tape can be produced by a computer, and this tape can then be used on a tape-controlled typewriter to give printed output. In some early computers this was the principal means of obtaining a printed output. A typical punching speed is 110 characters a second.

Punched cards are sometimes needed for re-input to the computer, and a computer card punch works at speeds between 100 and 250 cards a minute.

The typewriter

The typewriter mentioned previously as an input device can be used also to print information. Its relatively slow speed precludes its widespread use for large amounts of data.

Graph-plotter

A digital-incremental plotter can be attached to a computer to produce graphs or drawings from coordinates stored within the computer. A common form of this device consists of a movable pen and paper rollers that move under computer control at speeds of up to 18,000 steps a minute. The plotting is accurate to within a hundredth of an inch.

Bar charts and histograms for commercial purposes can be produced satisfactorily and at a higher speed by the line printer.

Cathode-ray-tube displays

A cathode-ray tube can be used to display either data in character form or graphs and drawings. Since no mechanical moving parts are involved, the speed of response is almost instantaneous. It is useful in research work for solving equations, obtaining an almost immediate answer and then inserting new variables via the typewriter.

Input and output devices and the magnetic storage units such as magnetic tape are often collectively called computer *peripherals*. We must now consider the main store, arithmetic unit and control unit which are sometimes referred to as the *central processor* or CPU.

The main store

The main store is sometimes called the computer 'memory' and is used to store the program instructions, data and intermediate results. Computer storage can be considered in two parts: main storage in which the items are rapidly accessible but which is expensive and therefore limited in size, and auxiliary storage which is less rapidly accessible. The main store is often referred to as the *immediate access store* or IAS.

In the most common form of main storage, the information is stored on small ferrite rings or cores. This is referred to as *core storage*. Information stored therein is reduced to a binary pattern that varies from one computer to another. Since a detailed knowledge of binary representation of information and instructions is not required when using the high-level programming languages described in this book, no further mention will be made of binary representation or binary arithmetic. The interested reader is referred to the programming manual of a particular computer for details of the representation of information inside that computer.

The individual cores are grouped into units to hold a unit of information that is referred to (depending on the particular computer) as a *word*, a *character*, a *slab* or a *byte*. The amount of information which can be held in one of these units varies considerably between computers, and details can be found in the appropriate programming manual. Data which are being transferred to or from a unit of store are automatically checked for any malfunction that would result in a digit being lost or gained. The computer store can be regarded as a series of compartments, each containing a word (or appropriate unit) of information. Each compartment can be considered as having an unique number, or *address*, which is referred to by program instructions when it is desired to deposit or retrieve information. The access time of a unit of storage is short; one microsecond is typical. These compartments are sometimes referred to as *locations* or *cells*.

Auxiliary storage devices

Since immediate access storage is costly, it would be prohibitive to use it to store the large files of records that are essential to commercial data processing. These records are usually held in some form of auxiliary store or backing store whilst the instructions of the program, working area and the single record currently being processed are held in the core store.

In scientific programming, the auxiliary store is often used to hold intermediate results and to transfer information from one program to another, since reading to and from auxiliary storage devices is much quicker than the corresponding operations with punched cards or paper tape. Frequently-used programs are invariably held in the auxiliary storage since they can thus be read into store much quicker than if they were stored on any other input medium.

Magnetic tape

The most usual form of auxiliary storage is magnetic tape. It may have been wondered why this was not discussed in the previous section on input devices. There are machines available that will produce a computer-readable magnetic tape as a byproduct of typing and these are coming into increasing use. However, the majority of magnetic tapes read by a computer have first to be written by a computer. If it is desired to create a file of commercial records on magnetic tape it is necessary first to read them into a computer, after they have been punched on cards or paper tape, and then write them onto magnetic tape.

Magnetic tape resembles the tape used in audio tape recorders. The most common width is half an inch; reels of tape may contain up to 800 metres. After it has been recorded, information is permanent on a magnetic tape until overwritten with new information.

The rate of information transfer to and from magnetic tape varies with particular computers from 5000 to 350,000 characters per second; malfunctions are automatically detected. Each computer has its own code for character representation on magnetic tape; only rarely can tape produced by one computer be read by another.

Many computers use six tape units (often referred to as *decks* or *handlers*). More units are often theoretically possible. Thus magnetic-tape auxiliary storage can be considered as an infinitely expandable store. When the information on one reel of tape has been used by a program, another can be put in the same tape deck, and the process can be repeated as often as desired. Often large commercial files, such as sales ledgers, occupy more than one reel of tape.

The most important limitation of magnetic-tape storage lies in the fact that work must be processed in the same sequence as the records are held on the tape. This can be a disadvantage as it can take considerable time to search for a record at the very end of a magnetic tape. Because of this need for sequential processing, magnetic tape is often referred to as a *serial-access* storage medium. Use of magnetic-tape files requires the input to be sorted in the same order as the file that the input updates, and in many commercial computer installations much computer time is devoured by this necessity to sort the input. It was once estimated that 40 per cent of computer time in Britain was spent in sorting data.

If it is desired to update a file without sorting and without the necessity of examining all records in a previous file, then some random-access storage device must be used instead of magnetic tape. Some forms of random-access auxiliary storage will now be considered.

Random-access storage

The most common form of random-access storage is the magnetic-disc unit, commonly known as a *disc drive*. Packs of discs, usually six, which contain 10 surfaces on which recording can be made, can be inserted in the drive. They are mounted on a continuously revolving shaft, and there are read/write heads for each surface.

A typical disc pack has a capacity of 7.25 million bytes. Average access time is 85 milliseconds, and the transfer rate is 156,000 characters a second. The average access time should be compared with the time needed to find a record half-way through a reel of tape.

Non-exchangeable disc and drum stores are also used as a random-access auxiliary storage. A typical drum store has an average access time of 10 milliseconds.

Another fairly common form of random-access device is the magnetic card. Data are recorded on magnetic cards made of a similar material to magnetic tape. These cards are held in a pack (or cartridge), and a single card can be speedily released on to a rotating drum when it is desired to read or write information on that individual card. Changing cartridges of magnetic cards is a speedier operation than the insertion of a magnetic tape into a tape deck. A typical transfer rate for one of these devices is 80,000 characters a second. This has the lowest cost per character stored of all random-access systems.

Buffer storage

The wide disparity between input/output speeds and the fantastic computing speeds will have been noticed. Early operators tolerated this lack of balance, and the computing units were idle for the lengthy periods of transfer to and from peripheral devices.

It is usual now to have special stores called *buffers* attached to input/output devices. When for instance a printer is requested by the program, the data are transferred at electronic speed from the main store to the appropriate peripheral buffer. The program can then continue computing whilst the printer takes its information from the buffer. Naturally if another print instruction is given before the buffer is empty, the program will stop until that particular buffer is free. More sophisticated computing systems have a 'pool' of buffers for all peripherals instead of attaching one buffer to one peripheral.

The arithmetic and control units

The arithmetic unit consists of the circuitry that performs the arithmetic and often a series of special registers or stores to hold operands and intermediate and final results of the computation. Many computers have a special register known as the *accumulator* in which the final result of an arithmetic operation is held.

Computers used for scientific and mathematical work usually have separate arithmetic circuitry for *fixed-point* and *floating-point* arithmetic. In fixed-point arithmetic, there is a fixed number of digits with which the arithmetic circuitry can deal. This means that very large and very small numbers cannot be represented; often it is inconvenient and difficult to arrange a calculation so that all numbers are within range. The decimal point is assumed wherever the programmer wishes, and, in long computations involving multiplication and division, this involves much laborious effort to keep track of the decimal point and to scale operands adequately in attempts to guard against loss of desired precision.

To overcome the problem of scaling, floating-point number representation is usually used for mathematical work. A number represented in floating-point form has two parts: an exponent and an argument. If n represents the desired number, a the argument, b the exponent and c the base, then

$$n = a \cdot c^b$$

The base is usually 10, 2 or 8, and it is usual to have the standard form of the argument as a fraction so that with a base of 2 typical representations would be as shown below:

number	exponent	argument
1	1	0.5
240	8	0.9375
−0.078125	−3	−0.625

so that

$$1 = 0.5 \times 2^1 = 0.5 \times 2$$
$$240 = 0.9375 \times 2^8 = 0.9375 \times 256$$
$$-0.078125 = -0.625 \times 2^{-3} = -0.625 \times 0.125$$

Since the exponent and argument together only occupy the same number of digits as a fixed-point number, it can be seen that a wider range of numbers can be represented within the limit of a fixed number of digits. The use of floating-point arithmetic saves the programmer the tiresome chore of keeping track of the point. Some numbers of course cannot be exactly represented in floating-point form (such as one-third or one-seventh), and the precision to which each computer works in floating-point form can be ascertained from the appropriate programming manual.

There is considerable variety in the arithmetic instructions built into computers. Some have only optional floating-point circuitry; others have no multiply or divide circuitry, whilst a few have built-in functions for such mathematical operations as the calculation of square roots and natural logarithms.

The control unit interprets each instruction in its proper sequence and initiates signals to the appropriate circuitry to perform the instructions. It may be considered the nerve centre of the whole computing system.

2

INTRODUCTION TO COMPUTER PROGRAMMING

The dependence of a computer upon its program has been stressed in the previous chapter. Without a program, a computer is little more than a bundle of wires and transistors, and whatever the program instruction commands the computer will endeavour to obey. A program consists of a detailed sequence of instructions for the computer to obey in order to perform a desired computation.

The steps in transferring a problem to the computer are:

1. Defining the problem. In commercial work, where the problem is often the transfer of a complicated system such as sales accounting to a computer, the problem definition falls into the scope of systems analysis and is not usually performed by the programmer. The systems analyst has to see exactly what is done in the pre-computer office system, design a computerized system to meet the objectives defined by management and supervise the implementation of this computerized system. In that case, the systems analyst gives a programmer a program specification containing a full definition of the problem. In scientific programming the definition of the problem should include investigation of the most appropriate numerical technique for the computation and full treatment of error conditions which may arise.
2. Preparing a method of solving the problem on a computer. Usually a programmer does not begin by writing instructions in a computer language but writes in some detail the steps necessary to solve the problem in order to arrive at a feasible logical solution that can be then translated into the desired computer language. This writing down of the steps is usually accomplished by flowcharting which will be discussed in the next section.
3. Writing the program itself in a computer language.
4. Providing data to test the program fully and compare the results given by the computer with the known results for the test input data. Programs are almost invariably incorrect in their first version and often need considerable testing or development before they can be considered suitably operational.
5. Documenting the program fully in such a way that any suitable person in the organization for which the program was written can understand the method of solution used in the program.

11

Flowcharting

A flowchart is a graphic description of the steps needed in solving a problem. It is a vital step in organizing the ideas of the programmer and is essential for communication between the computer personnel and the rest of the skilled staff. A flowchart is relatively simple for a layman to understand, whereas the full implication of a program can be grasped only by a person with some background knowledge of the programming language used.

4. A rectangular box represents a simple step in the program; a diamond-shaped box represents a decision with two exits

Each step in a flowchart is written in a *box* (Fig. 4). The various shapes of the boxes have been standardized (B.S. 4058). Only two of the standard shapes are normally necessary: the rest of the shapes are for the systems flowcharts drawn up by systems analysts. The rectangular box is for a step or process in the computation. The diamond-shaped box has two exits and is for a decision.

Fig. 5 shows a simple flowchart needed to read three numbers from paper tape and to print their average.

The degree of detail in the wording inside each box is determined by ease of communication. A flowchart should be written in such a way that it can be understood by any person who is likely to need some acquaintance with the method used. The flowchart of Fig. 5 uses fairly detailed wording. If a similar flowchart was being prepared for use only by programmers we could replace *read number from tape* in the third box by *read n*.

Complicated flowcharts usually begin with boxes of broad detail, and then a second flowchart is drawn up in which each of the original boxes is divided into steps of greater detail. In a flowchart with broad detail all the steps of the flowchart above could be described in one box as *read numbers and print average*. Sometimes more than two levels of detail are used; an organization usually sets its own standards here.

In Fig. 5 it will be observed that steps 3 and 4 are repeated three times, and if it was desired to read 100 numbers and calculate their average these steps would have to be repeated 100 times. To avoid this, programs are usually conceived as being a series of *loops*. The flowchart in Fig. 6 shows the same problem done for 100 numbers using a loop. It will be noticed that two alternative versions of the flowchart are given. Rarely in either programming or flowcharting is there a unique correct solution: in a complicated problem many equally correct versions of a solution can be found.

The concept of a loop can be generalized in the following steps.

1. Set counter to zero.
2. Perform process.
3. Add one to counter.
4. If counter is less than desired value go to step 2.
5. (Exit from loop.)

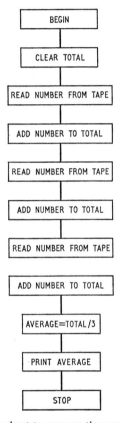

5. Flowchart to average three numbers

Sometimes in mathematical work it is desired to repeat a calculation until sufficient accuracy has been achieved, after which the loop is left. Instead of a counter being tested to see if it is necessary to repeat the loop, this kind of loop includes a test as to whether the desired accuracy has been achieved. The flowchart shown in Fig. 7 is to find the square root of a number, n, read from paper tape, by an iterative method. It uses the

fact that, if x is an approximation to the square root, a better approximation, s, is given by

$$s = \frac{1}{2}\left(x + \frac{n}{x}\right)$$

The flowchart gives x an arbitrary starting value of 1. Since it is desired
to evaluate the square root, s, to ten figures, the loop will continue to be
obeyed until $|x - s| < 0.0000000001s$.

Sometimes the number of times it is desired to execute a loop varies
each time the program is obeyed. If it was desired to print the average
of a number of observations which varied each day, one could not set a
number to terminate the loop since a different number of observations

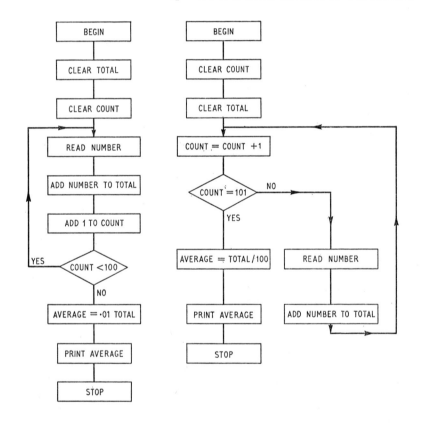

FIRST VERSION   SECOND VERSION

6. Two flowcharts for averaging a hundred numbers

would be recorded each day. In such a case the data are terminated with a character which would *not* normally occur in the data and which is called a *sentinel.* If the data are always positive, an ideal sentinel would be −1.

The flowchart of Fig. 8 illustrates the computation of the means of three sets of numbers each of which ends with a sentinel of −1. It illustrates a loop within a loop.

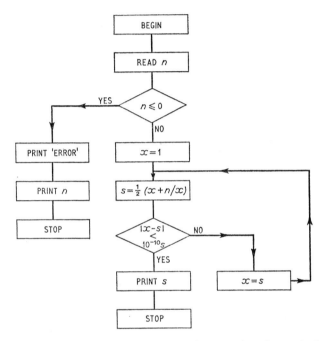

7. Flow chart to find the square root of n by an iterative method.

So far in the flowcharts for the computation of the average, the numbers have not been preserved in the computer store after they have been read from the tape and added to the total. If the numbers were being preserved they could be considered as a *set* or *array* of numbers. Mathematically, members of such a set are represented by using *suffices* or *subscripts*. A variable in such a set is often referred to as a *subscripted variable* such as $a_1, a_2, ..., a_n$. A member of an array is known as an *element*.

Arrays often use more than one subscript; an array with n subscripts is known as n-dimensional array. A two-dimensional array with rows and columns like a table is known as a *matrix*. In a matrix, the variable $a_{2,3}$ would refer to the third column of the second row. The elements of a matrix with three rows and four columns can be represented as:

$$
\begin{array}{cccc}
a_{1,1} & a_{1,2} & a_{1,3} & a_{1,4} \\
a_{2,1} & a_{2,2} & a_{2,3} & a_{2,4} \\
a_{3,1} & a_{3,2} & a_{3,3} & a_{3,4}
\end{array}
$$

The flowchart in Fig. 9 illustrates the addition of two matrices A and B of three rows and four columns to produce a third matrix C. The use of subscripted variables enables loops to be used to perform operations on each variable in turn in a systematic manner.

Often a section of program such as the solution of a set of equations may be required in several different places in a program. To write the

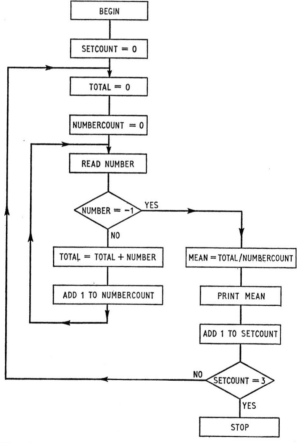

8. Flowchart incorporating a loop within a loop. It finds the means of three sets

section out in full whenever required would be wasteful: the concept of a *subroutine* enables the section to be written once only and to let the program call the section whenever needed. A subroutine will always return to the main program immediately after the instruction which called it.

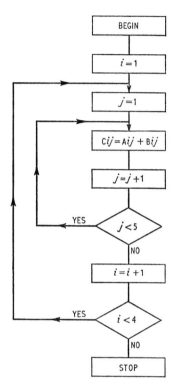

9. Addition of two matrices

The flowchart shown in Fig. 10 illustrates the use of a subroutine. It is desired to read ten amounts, print each amount, ascertain if it is divisible by 7, print their total and whether this is divisible by 7 and also their mean and if this is divisible by 7. Thus it is necessary to use a subroutine at three different places on the program.

Once written, a subroutine can be used in many different programs. Computer manufacturers supply subroutines in various computer languages for common computations such as income-tax calculation, statistical computations and matrix manipulation.

Program testing and development

After the problem is flowcharted to the required level of detail, it is written in the appropriate computer language. Programs are rarely successful at the first attempt, and the development of a program until it is ready to be classed as operational may take some time.

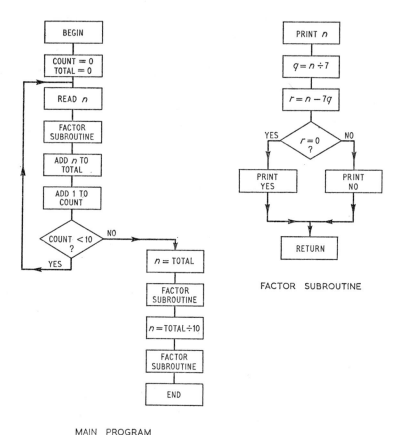

MAIN PROGRAM

FACTOR SUBROUTINE

10. Use of a subroutine

The high cost of computer time makes it essential for a program to be fully tested with trial data before it is ever tried on the computer. This pre-computer testing should be by no means underestimated as pounds of computer time may be saved. Since a programmer tends to be infatuated by his own creations, the testing should, if practicable, be done by another programmer.

The test data should test every branch in the program including the error conditions. In some commercial data-processing installations, the test data are supplied by the systems analyst. When the testing away from the computer is satisfactorily completed, the program can then be transferred to the computer. Naturally the punched copy of the program should be carefully examined for transcription errors before it is submitted to the computer. When a program is being tested on a computer, three types of error can arise:

1. 'Grammatical' errors. These arise when a mistake is made in writing the particular language used so that the computer cannot recognize what the instruction means. If there is a grammatical error, the program will not be obeyed at all. The computer usually prints out information about the position and nature of the error so that it can be easily corrected.

2. Sometimes when the program is being executed, the computer stops because the program asks for some instruction to be obeyed which cannot be sensibly done, e.g. it asks the tape reader to read a number when there is no tape in the reader. Some computers will stop if any attempt is made to divide into or by zero or to extract the square root of a negative number. Usually a message is printed out which identifies the error condition.

3. Logical errors. The program sometimes runs to the end and gives erroneous results or enters an endless loop. This means that although the computer obeyed the instructions faithfully, the instructions did not provide a correct solution to the problem.

Various diagnostic routines are supplied by computer manufacturers to assist programmers whose programs fall into the last type of error. Common 'debugging' (as elimination of errors is called) aids include a program (known as a *memory dump*) to print out the computer store at the end of the program, and programs which print out certain parts of the store each time certain instructions are obeyed. The manufacturers' programming manuals give full details of these diagnostic routines. Judicious and careful use of these facilities will save much time in the testing and development of programs.

3

COMPUTER LANGUAGES

A set of instructions for a computer must be written in one of the many "computer languages" Basically computer languages are of two types: the instruction code built into a particular computer (*machine instructions*) and *automatic programming language* or *autocode*, which is more like English or mathematical notation but which requires to be translated by the computer into machine instructions before it can be obeyed. Machine instructions are often known as *machine code*. Although the rest of this book deals with automatic programming languages, a short discussion of machine code will not be out of place here. Interested readers who wish to pursue the subject further must have recourse to the appropriate machine-code programming manual.

Machine instructions

A machine instruction basically consists of a numerical function code and the address of the unit of the computer store on which the desired function is to be performed. For example, on one computer:

001800   means *put the contents of store location 800 to the accumulator*.
004801   means *subtract the contents of store location 801 from the accumulator*.

The number and power of machine instructions vary considerably from one computer to another. There are four main types of machine instruction:

1. Arithmetical.
2. Transfer instructions, which take data from one part of the store to another and to and from the accumulator and similar registers.
3. Logical instructions, which allow the normal sequence of the program to be broken if a certain condition is present. These are the kind of instruction that would be represented by a diamond-shaped box in a flowchart.
4. Input, output and auxiliary store instructions.

Below is a small section of program for one computer written in machine code. It is desired to perform the operation

$k = i+j$
(i is stored in location 800 and j in 801).

001800   put i to the accumulator,
003801   add j,
002802   store the result in k

Thus, for a comparatively trivial operation, three instructions are needed. It is obvious that machine instructions bear no resemblance to any other form of communication and are unintelligible to the uninitiated. With a few exceptions every computer has a different machine code from the others. The above section of program in the machine language of the IBM 1620 computer would be:

```
22 00500 00500   clear k,
21 00500 00520   add i to k,
21 00500 00540   add j to k
```

(i is stored in location 520 and j in location 540)

The re-programming which would be involved in the transfer of a program from one computer to another is one reason why machine code is not often used for programs now.

The detail inseparable from it, which causes many data-processing programs to contain many thousands of instructions, is another factor that militates against the use of machine code. Since the individual instructions in machine language accomplish so little, the length of programs means a higher error ratio. Machine-language programs are lengthy to write and develop. The training of programmers is lengthy since both a logical mind and a meticulous attention to clerical detail are required.

Since machine language is not, for the above reasons, a convenient notation for writing programs, more and more programs are now written in some kind of autocode, which the computer has first to translate into its own machine instructions. Autocode programming helps to surmount the language barrier between man and computer.

Assembly languages

Assembly languages are still close to machine code and are usually written for a particular computer, which means that in the majority of cases re-programming is necessary if another computer is used or acquired.

An assembly language, like all computer languages except the machine instructions of a particular computer, requires translation. The computer itself performs the translation as its accuracy and speed make it suitable for this kind of work (computers are also used for translating one human language into another). The process of running a program written in anything except machine code is:

1. The computer language program is written and punched.
2. A translating program known as the *compiler* (or *assembler*) is read into the computer. This then treats the computer language program as data and translates it into the appropriate machine code.
3. The resulting machine-code program is then obeyed.

The original computer program is often known as the *source program* and the resulting machine-code program is known as the *object program*. During the process of compilation some intermediate languages between source program and object program may be used.

The process of compilation can be compared to a reader first making a complete translation of a novel in a foreign language before reading it. The compiler can be thought of as a combined dictionary and grammar for translating the source program into the object program. Each source-program statement is analysed for syntactical correctness before translation. Compilers are normally provided by the computer manufacturer and are possibly the most specialized and intricate programs to write and represent a great deal of money.

A compiler for an assembly language is often known as an *assembler*. An instruction in assembly language (sometimes called a *symbolic* assembly language) often consists of a mnemonic function code followed by either a symbolic address or an actual machine address.

In the two types of assembly language a program to represent

$$k = i + j$$

would be:

1.   LDA I   put I to accumulator,
     ADD J   add J,
     STA K   store result in K
2.   LDA 500   put i to accumulator,
     ADD 501   add j,
     STA 502   store result in k

It can be seen that there is here a one-for-one correspondence with machine code. Some assembly languages contain more powerful statements known as *macros*. These are statements that give rise to many machine-language instructions; they are most commonly used for input and output procedures as some computers have only machine-code instructions to read and print one character at a time. Some assemblers allow the programmer the facility to write his own macros; these are very useful for mathematical functions like the computation of logarithms.

It is much quicker to write and develop programs in assembly language than in machine code. If symbolic addresses can be used, the programmer is relieved of the tiresome chore of allocating storage.

The chief virtue (and probably greatest limitation) of an assembly language is that it takes full advantage of the merits in design of an individual computer. This unfortunately implies that, on the rare occasions when an assembly-language program can be compiled on a computer different from the one for which it was originally created, the resulting object program will rarely be efficient.

Assembly time for assembly languages is usually short since the majority of instructions have a one-for-one correspondence with machine languages. Therefore translation into machine language is not a very lengthy or complicated process.

Common assembly languages in current use in Britain are the IBM System 360 Symbolic Assembler, PLAN (ICL 1900 Series), NEAT (ICL 4100 Series), Usercode (ICL System 4) and the City and Guilds Mnemonic Code.

High-level computer languages

High-level languages are primarily problem-oriented. It will have been noticed that, though assembly languages are more easily comprehensible than machine language, they are still very far from English or mathematical notation. The purpose behind the development of high-level computer languages was to enable a programmer to write his program in something close to English or mathematical notation and to let the computer perform the translation into machine code. The vast gap between assembly language and high-level language can be seen in the three following versions of the statement

$$k = i + j$$

which can be compared with the machine language and assembly language versions in the previous sections of this chapter.

$k := i + j;$	(Algol)
$K = I + J$	(Fortran)
ADD I TO J GIVING K	(Cobol)

It can be seen that such statements are more immediately intelligible than any encountered in the previous sections of this chapter and that training programmers in such languages takes a much shorter time. Such languages take no account of the individual excellencies of a particular computer; most computers have a compiler for at least two of the languages mentioned above. The aim of the designers of a high-level language is to create a language free from syntactical ambiguities that can be expressed in the character set of the majority of computers and that resembles English or mathematical notation.

All human languages contain many syntactical ambiguities such as the three meanings in the English sentence

time flies like an arrow.

Apart from the obvious meaning where *time* is the subject of the verb *flies*, there is a possible meaning (analogous to *fruit flies like a banana*) where *time* is an adjective, and a third meaning where *time* is an imperative verb.

Computer programs have been written which can syntactically analyse sentences and identify the alternatives, but no technique has yet been perfected which will resolve semantic ambiguities of human languages. Therefore any existing human language would be highly unsuitable as a high-level computer language, and one must not therefore repine if a Cobol program has not the immediate readability or the aesthetic qualities of a Jane Austen novel!

Algol, Fortran and Cobol have been implemented on a wide variety of computers, and the newer computer language PL/I is being implemented on some computers. The concept of a language not tied to a particular computer is known as *machine independence* (sometimes unkindly referred to as a myth). It is very unlikely that a program in Algol, Fortran or Cobol can be transferred from one computer to another without some minor alterations. Algol input/output facilities differ considerably from one computer to another; Fortran has many dialects whilst Cobol has many 'elective features' which may or may not be implemented for a given computer. Not all high-level languages are machine-independent. Some very good and effective high-level languages are implemented by a single computer manufacturer such as the Honeywell FACT, N.C.R.'s Language H and the I.C.L. CLEO. New languages are constantly being developed such as BCL, which is a general-purpose computer language developed by the University of London Institute of Computer Science and which contains some interesting and unique features.

Since high-level language is so far removed from machine language, it will be understood that it cannot be translated as quickly as an assembly language and the object program may be more inefficient in its use of the computer store. For many users, however, the ease with which a high-level language program can be written more than compensates for this slight inefficiency.

Until the advent of PL/I, high-level programming languages were considered as either scientific languages or commercial data-processing languages. Algol, Fortran and Mercury Autocode were examples of the former whilst Cobol and the manufacturers' data-processing languages such as CLEO were examples of the latter. It was always possible to use one kind of language to do the work of the other kind; until efficient Cobol compilers became common, some data processing was done in Fortran. Yet writing a scientific program in Cobol has been aptly, if unkindly, compared to shelling peas in boxing gloves.

Until PL/I was conceived, some computer systems dealt with the problem of data-processing applications requiring much statistical computation by allowing a Cobol program to use Fortran for the more mathematical parts. Entry into machine code for computations outside the scope of high-level language such as the reading of punched cards and tape in unusual codes has invariably been allowed in manufacturers' compilers.

There are some high-level programming languages for special purposes which are outside the scope of this book. Examples are APT for the numerical control of machine tools and Simscript for operational-research problems involving simulation techniques.

4

ALGOL 60

Algol is the most elegant and logical of all the high-level programming languages. It was devised by an international committee as a vehicle for the communication of algorithms and the first version was produced in 1958. The current version of the language is usually referred to as Algol 60. The language is maintained by the International Federation for Information Processing.

The language has a strong appeal to mathematicians who can describe the steps of a computation in a reasonably readable way that is suitable for instructing a computer. A relatively large number of Algol programs or algorithms have been published in various journals.† The reader interested in numerical methods is referred to these publications as there is a probability that his problem already has a suitable published program. Indeed more programs have been published in Algol than in any other computer language. Access is therefore gained to a wide variety of expert techniques in the field of numerical analysis.

Since Algol is used on many different types of computers and is meant to be independent of any particular kind of punching equipment, three versions of the language have been defined:

1. *Reference Algol*: This is the language as defined by the Algol report and is used in most published programs. It contains 116 basic symbols including some which are not usually found on punching equipment such as $\wedge$ (and), $\neg$ (not).

2. *Publication Algol*: This contains characters and notations that are not in the reference language if they can be converted to reference-language representation. The result is often very close to mathematical notation; Greek letters and normal index notation can be used.

3. *Hardware representation*: Since the full Algol character set does not appear on many punching machines, the hardware representation for a particular computer shows how certain basic symbols are actually represented. For example:
On the ICT 1900 series,

$\wedge$ is represented as <u>and</u>

† *Communications of the Association for Computing Machinery* (U.S.A.); *The Computer Journal, The Computer Bulletin* (Britain); *Numerische Mathematik* (Germany); *Algorytmy* (U.S.S.R.).

In some punched card versions of Algol,

    $=$ is represented as 'EQ'

Basic symbols

Algol programs are composed in the basic symbols of the language. Below is a list of these; their meaning will be explained in the course of this chapter.

1. Upper case (capital) and lower case (small) English letters.
2. The digits 0 to 9.
3. The logical values **true** and **false**.
4. Delimiters.

(a) Operators

Arithmetic	Relational	Logical	Sequential
$+$	$>$	$\vee$	**goto**
$-$	$\geqslant$	$\wedge$	**if**
$\uparrow$	$=$	$\equiv$	**then**
$/$	$<$	$\supset$	**else**
$\times$	$\leqslant$	$\neg$	**for**
$\div$	$\neq$		**do**

(b) Separators

,	;	**step**	**comment**
.	$:=$	**until**	10
:	⌴	**while**	

(c) Brackets

⌐ ¬	]	
(	**begin**	
)	**end**	
[		

(d) Declarators

own	**procedure**
Boolean	**switch**
integer	**label**
real	**string**
array	**value**

It will be seen that certain basic symbols are always printed in bold-face type. Those above are the symbols of the reference language. For punching conventions in the various hardware representations, the reader is referred to the Algol programming manual of the particular computer used. Insertion of blank spaces and new lines makes no difference to an

Algol program, so that a program can be written in a format which is readily comprehensible.

```
a   v   e   r
        a
            g
    e
```

is an acceptable (if eccentric) way of writing average.

Variable names

Variable names are the chief kind of Algol identifiers for naming some item in the program as the programmer wishes. The reader will recollect that this is a very convenient method of referring to individual units of the computer store.

A variable name is a string of letters or digits commencing with a letter. In theory there is no restriction on the length of an identifier; in practice various compilers impose restrictions here, and details can be found in the appropriate programming manual.

Bold-face letters *cannot* be used for an identifier.

Acceptable identifiers are

x	B50d
Y	sindy
gg	Alison
average	item1
a4	WEIGHT

Unacceptable identifiers would be

1stmean	(starts with a numeral)
π	(a Greek letter)
y7.3	(contains character not a letter or number)

Theoretically, names should be used to make the meaning of a program clear to a reader. The tendency (especially among those who punch their own programs) to relapse into a series of single character names or to use esoteric names should be avoided.

It must be remembered that capital and small letters refer to different identifiers.

Type declarations

Each variable name must have its type declared before it is used. In simple programs this is done at the beginning of the program. The two most common type declarations are

integer and **real.**

The former is used if a variable name is to contain a whole number. Variables are declared as type **real** if they might contain a fractional part. **real** variables are held in floating-point form which was explained in chapter 1 under *The Arithmetic and Control Units.* The appropriate programming manual should be consulted for the range of numbers which can be held in **real** and **integer** variables.

The general form of a type declaration is:

type   variable-name 1, variable-name 2, ..., variable-name n;

so that typical type declarations could be

integer   item, n, count;
real   sum, mean, x;

It is immaterial whether **integer** or **real** variables are declared first, and the order in which individual variables are declared needs bear no relation to the order in which they are used in a program. The same variable name must not be used for an **integer** and a **real** variable. (There are exceptions to this, but the beginner should avoid them; see *Block Structure* on page 45.)

The compiler will reject as faulty any program containing a variable name that has not been previously declared (Fortran programmers, please note!).

Numerical constants

Numbers are classified into **real** and **integer** types according to the form in which they are written. If a number contains only the symbols − + and the digits 0–9 then it is of type **integer**: otherwise it is type **real** as the following examples show:

Type **integer**   +17   −654   452   073   0
Type **real**   +17.865   −654.23   0.765   .873   −.76   .62   17.0

Since the emphasis is on the written form of a number, 17.0 is of type **real** even though it is a whole number. The distinction between **real** and **integer** constants is especially important in connection with the operators ↑ and ÷ (see below). Elsewhere it is immaterial. The + sign is optional and insignificant zeros are ignored.

A number must not end with a decimal point.

To avoid writing strings of zeros for very large and very small numbers, a decimal exponent form can be used. Numbers written in this manner are of type **real.**

In this method the exponent of each number is specified as the appropriate *integral* power of 10. Thus

$$.451_{10}-3 = .451 \times 10^{-3} = .000451$$
$$12.76_{10}4 = 12.76 \times 10^4 = 127,600$$
$$_{10}5 = \qquad 10^5 = 100,000$$
$$-_{10}5 = \qquad -10^5 = -100,000$$
$$_{10}-5 = \qquad 10^{-5} = .00001$$
$$_{10}+5 = \qquad 10^5 = 100,000$$

Fractional powers of 10 are not allowed to be expressed in this particular form so that $15.6_{10}3.5$ would be unacceptable. The symbol $_{10}$ is *not* an arithmetic operator.

Simple arithmetic expressions

The simplest arithmetic expression is sometimes known as an assignment statement. This inserts a value into a variable, e.g.

    pi:=3.14;   sum:=0;   total:=items;

It can be seen that the right-hand part of an assignment statement can be either a variable or a constant.

Mixed **integer** and **real** types are allowed in arithmetic expressions. If an expression of type **integer** is inserted into a **real** variable, then the result is held in the computer in floating-point form.

If a **real** expression is stored in an integer variable, then the value is converted to **integer** form.

If n has been declared as an integer variable:

    n:=5.2;   (n contains 5)
    n:=5.8;   (n contains 6)
    n:=-5.4;   (n contains -5)
    n:=-5.7;   (n contains -6)

It cannot be emphasized too strongly (especially to Fortran programmers) that the assignment separator is := and *not* =. An expression such as d = g; would not be recognized as an assignment statement, and the program would be faulted. It will also be noticed that each statement ends with a semi-colon.

A multiple assignment statement is allowed for variables which are all the same type, e.g.

    n:=m:=i:=8;

This inserts the value 8 in n, m and i. If these three variables were not all of the same type the program would be faulted.

Variables and constants may be combined by the arithmetic operators to form more complicated assignment statements.

Addition is represented by $+$
Subtraction by $-$
Multiplication by $*$
(throughout this chapter, $*$ is the usual hardware representation of the multiplication sign, which rarely appears in punching equipment).

Multiplication is never implicit. The statement

n:=ab;

would put the value of an identifier ab (if one has been declared) into n. It would not insert the product of a and b.

There are two division operators, / and $\div$.

The operator / is the division symbol normally used and gives a **real** result so that

a:=7/3;

would put 2.3333333... in a.

The operator $\div$ can only be used with operands of type **integer**; it gives an **integer** result *rounded towards zero*.

$7 \div 3$ has an **integer** value of 2
$17 \div 9$ has an **integer** value of 1
$-7 \div 3$ has an **integer** value of -2
$-17 \div 9$ has an **integer** value of -1

$7 \div 2.0$ and $900 \div_{10} 2$ are illegal as they contain **real** constants.

The operator $\uparrow$ denotes exponentiation. n $\uparrow$ m denotes n^m. An **integer** result is given only when n is type **integer** and m is type **integer** and positive or zero. Otherwise the result is **real**. No values of base or exponent which would given infinite, indeterminate or imaginary results are allowed. If the exponent is **real** the value of the base must never be negative. Plain round brackets, ( ), can be used to any depth, and redundant brackets are invariably ignored.

An arithmetic expression is evaluated from left to right unless the adjacent operator has a higher priority as indicated in the following list:

first $\uparrow$
second $/ \div *$
third $+ -$

Brackets may be used to override the above order of evaluation.

$p + q \div r + s$ means $p + (q \div r) + s$
x/y/z   means x/yz

Algol follows the practice of normal algebraic notation in not writing two operators together.

a+(−b)   is the correct version of a+ −b
d/(−e)   is the correct version of d/−e
h ↑ (−k)   is the correct version of h ↑−k

The reader is reminded especially to guard against a fault like this last example. It is often forgotten that the various hardware representations of ↑ are really operators.

Standard functions

The power of an arithmetic expression can be increased by the inclusion of the standard functions listed below. The argument of a standard function is an arithmetic expression (which can include another function), and the argument must *always* be enclosed in plain parentheses. In this list X stands for any arithmetic expression.

Real functions

abs(X)	the absolute value or modulus of X
arctan(X)	the principal value (in radians) of the inverse tangent of X between $-\pi/2$ and $\pi/2$
cos(X)	the cosine of X radians
exp(X)	the exponential function of X (e^X)
ln(X)	the natural logarithm of X
sin(X)	the sine of X radians
sqrt(X)	the square root of X

Integer functions

sign(X)   the sign of the value of X
             +1 if X>0
             0 if X = 0
             −1 if X<0

entier(X)   the largest integer *not greater than* X
             entier(5.4) = 5
             entier(5.9) = 5
             entier(−5.4) = −6
             entier(−5.9) = −6

All except experienced Algol programmers should avoid using the names of the standard functions for their own purposes (see the section on *Functions* later in this chapter for a further discussion of this).

Input and output facilities

The Algol report specifies no input/output procedures. The implementation of such procedures is left to the designers of individual compilers. As it is rarely possible to have realistic programming examples without recourse to such facilities, this chapter will introduce the procedures used in ICL Atlas Algol which are also implemented in ICL 1900 series Algol. The reader is referred to the Algol manual for the particular computer used.

Input

The standard function 'read' provides the value of the next number from the chosen input. This function will only read numbers that may be terminated on the paper tape by two consecutive spaces, a newline character, a comma or a semi-colon. Single spaces are everywhere ignored. A typical printout of a data tape would be

```
1.2      2.3
-17.9    +7
```

If the following instructions were given:

```
a:=read;   b:=read;   c:=read;   d:=read;
```

a would contain 1.2, b 2.3, c −17.9 and d 7.

Output

A statement of the form

```
print(X, m, n)
```

where X is any arithmetic expression, prints the value of the expression X in a style determined by m and n. As a general rule beginners will not want to give m the value of zero, and the effect of this will not be discussed.

m determines the number of places it is desired to print before the decimal point. If the number is larger than the number of places requested before the point, the entire number is still printed without loss of significant digits. n determines the number of places printed after the point. The number is rounded on the next place, e.g. the instruction print(a, 3, 4) when a = 234.5678535 would print

234.5679

The number is preceded by a space if it is positive or by − if it is negative and is always followed by two spaces. Non-significant zeros are suppressed. If the number that it is desired to print is a fraction, the zero in the unit position is printed if the recommended form with m = 1 is used. For example, .075 would be printed as 0.075 with the print statement print(x, 1, 3). If n = 0, the number is rounded to the nearest integer and no decimal point is printed.

If more spaces are required, the instruction

space(n)

where n is an integer expression, will output n spaces.

If it is desired to print on a new line the instruction

newline (n)

where n is an integer expression, will output n newlines. newline(1) will print on the next line; newline(2) will print on the next line but one.

If one wants to print characters for titles, etc., the appropriate instruction is

writetext({TITLE})

This would print the word 'TITLE'.

Any string of characters which can be represented on the printer can be substituted for title. The hatched parentheses are a substitute in Atlas Algol for the Algol characters ⌐ and ⌐.

For further details on the input/output facilities for Atlas Algol, the reader is referred to *A Primer of Algol 60 Programming for the Atlas Computer* (ICL Ltd.).

Labels and goto statements

It is sometimes necessary for a program to go backwards or forwards to a certain statement. In order to identify a particular statement, a label is used.

A label is an identifier written before the statement to which it refers and separated from this statement by a colon. Normally a label is different from any other identifier used in the program. It is constructed according to the rules for identifier construction defined in the earlier section on *Variable Names*. A typical statement with a label is

start: n:=read;

In order to jump to any labelled statement a **goto** statement is used. It is of the form

goto k;

where k is a label, e.g.

goto start;

The uses of labels and **goto** statements will become clear after study of the next section.

if statements

A digital computer is capable of taking a decision and transferring control to a certain labelled part of the program according to the test it makes. All programs except the most trivial make use of this facility; indeed, examples in Algol have been postponed until now so that realistic problems may be undertaken.

A simple use of the **if** statement would be:

if h = 5 **then goto** next; a := u;

Here control would go to next if h was equal to 5, and the program would obey the statement labelled 'next' and instructions in sequence after that. If h ≠ 5, the program would omit the statement after **then** and start obeying statements beginning with the statement a := u;

The general form of the **if** statement can be represented as

if Boolean expression **then** unconditional statement;

A simple Boolean expression can be considered as being of the form:

simple arithmetic expression   relational operator   simple arithmetic expression.

A Boolean expression can possess only two possible values: true or false.

Relational operators are:

$$= \quad > \quad <$$
$$\neq \quad \geqslant \quad \leqslant$$

The relational operator must *never* be written := .

Some examples of simple Boolean expressions therefore are:

$$n = 5$$
$$a + b + c > \text{sqrt}(d/e)$$

Simple Boolean expressions can be combined to form more complicated Boolean expressions by means of Boolean operators. The most useful Boolean operators are:

∧   and
∨   or

Expressions using these operators are:

$$n \geqslant 4 \; \wedge \; n \leqslant 50$$
$$a = 6 \; \vee \; b = 8$$

These can be extremely useful when testing the allowed range of an item.

The relational operators = and ≠ should not be used when comparing expressions of type **real**, as two expressions that are thought to be equal may differ by a minute quantity owing to the floating-point representation of real quantities.

Instead of writing

if x = 31.7 **then goto** next;

one should write

if abs(x − 31.7) < $_{10}$ − 10 **then goto** next;

Any very small quantity which can be represented in a particular computer may be substituted for $_{10}$ − 10.

A complete program will now be presented. It is desired to read ten numbers from paper tape and to print their average. It will be noticed that a program commences with **begin** and concludes with **end**.

> **begin**
> **real** x, average, total; **integer** count;
> total : = 0; count : = 0;
> start: x : = read; total : = total + x; count : = count + 1;
> **if** count < 10 **then goto** start;
> average : = total/10; print(average, 4, 3)
> **end**

When a statement is followed by **end** the semi-colon can be omitted.

Compound statements

So far only one statement has been used after **then**. Sometimes it is desired to have a series of statements which will be obeyed if the Boolean expression after **if** is true. In this event the statements are bracketed together by a **begin** and an **end**. This is known as a compound statement.

In the following example it is desired to print a negative number on a newline (requiring two statements) and then to continue the main program.

if n < 0 **then begin** print(n, 3, 0); newline(1) **end**; n : = read;

It will be noticed that the semicolon after the compound statement is vital as it terminates the **if** statement.

A compound statement can be labelled before the **begin**.

A compound statement is defined to be unconditional, so **if** can follow **then** when the second **if** is preceded by a **begin**. For example,

if n = 4 **then begin if** m = 7 **then** print(p, 4, 0) **end**; a : = read;

If the **begin** and **end** were omitted here, the statement would be ambiguous as well as ungrammatical. A more elegant way of writing the same statement would be:

if n = 4 ∧ m = 7 **then** print(p, 4, 0); a : = read;

The **if then else** statement

This is the second type of conditional statement in Algol. It is used when one wants to perform one of two alternative statements according to the truth or falsity of a condition. It will be recalled that the **if then** statement only provided an alternative if the condition was true. The form is:

if Boolean expression **then** unconditional statement **else** statement;

The following examples will make clear the different uses of the two types of conditional statement.

if then *statement*

It is required to print a number only if it is positive and to do no printing if it is negative or zero, and then to proceed to read a number into x.

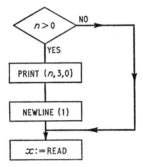

if n > 0 **then begin** print(n, 3, 0); newline (1) **end**; x : = read;

if then else *statement*

It is required to augment count1 if n is positive and count2 if it is negative or zero before reading a number into x.

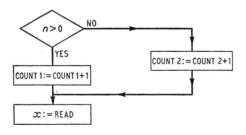

if n > 0 **then** count1 : = count1 + 1 **else** count2 : = count2 + 1; x : = read;

Naturally **then, else** or both can be followed by a compound statement **else** must *never* have a semi-colon immediately before it.

A judicious use of the **if then else** statement can eliminate many **goto** statements from a program.

Exercises 4.1†

1. Print the integers 1–100 with their square, cube, square root and cube root.
2. Compute and print the reciprocals of the numbers 2–100 to six decimal places.
3. Read in 12 sales amounts for the 12 months, and print each as a ratio to January with January = 100.
4. Read in ten pairs of numbers representing the smaller sides of ten right-angled triangles, and print the ten hypotenuse values.
5. Print a table of circles with areas increasing in steps of a square metre from 1 to 100 square metres and their corresponding radii. (Assume $\pi = 3.14$.)
6. $\pi/4 = 1 - \frac{1}{3} + \frac{1}{5} - \frac{1}{7} + \frac{1}{9}$. Evaluate 1000 terms of this series, and print out the value of π to eight decimal places every 100 terms.
7. Compute and print the terms of the Fibonacci series ($x_{n+1} = x_n + x_{n-1}$) between 10^5 and 10^8. The first few terms are 0 1 1 2 3 5 8....
8. The solution of the simultaneous equations

$$ax + by + c = 0$$
$$px + qy + r = 0$$

is given by

$$x = (br - cq)/(aq - bp)$$
$$y = (pc - ar)/(aq - bp)$$

Read a, b, c, p, q, r and compute and print x and y.
Print INDETERMINATE if $aq - bp = 0$.
Print NOT INDEPENDENT if $a/p = b/q = c/r$.

for statements

step–until *type*

All computer programs except the simplest and most trivial involve loops. The **for** statement gives a simpler method of expressing a loop than has been hitherto encountered with the **if–then** statement.

The following examples show the same program with and without a **for** statement. It is a program to print the squares and cubes of numbers between 1 and 100.

† Suggested solutions to all exercises follow after chapter 8.

(a)
```
begin real square; integer number;
number:=1;
start: print(number, 3, 0); square:=number * number;
        print(square, 6, 0); print(square * number, 9. 0); newline(1);
        number:=number+1; if number < 101 then goto start
end
```

(b)
```
begin real square; integer number;
   for number:=1 step 1 until 100 do
      begin print(number, 3, 0); square:=number * number;
            print(square, 6, 0); print(square * number, 9, 0);
            newline (1)
      end
end
```

The expression 1 **step** 1 **until** 100 is an example of a **for** list element. The **for** statement executes the statement (simple or compound) following **do** until all values in the sequence have been dealt with. The variable 'number' is known as the controlled variable. The statement following **do** is known as the range of the **for** statement.

A **for** list element of the **step until** type has the general form

A **step** B **until** C

where A, B and C are all arithmetic expressions, e.g.

a + b **step** sqrt(e − f) **until** g + h

The following examples show the sequences executed in various cases.

3 **step** 2 **until** 7	denoting the sequence 3, 5, 7
9 **step** − 2 **until** 5	denoting the sequence 9, 7, 5
1 **step** − 2 **until** − 5	denoting the sequence 1, − 1, − 3, − 5
1 **step** 2 **until** 8	denoting the sequence 1, 3, 5, 7

The last case is explained by the fact that when the increment is added after the execution of each part of the **step**, a test is made to see if the absolute value of the controlled variable is larger than the absolute value of the final value. If so the program jumps out of the range of the **for** statement.

In a case such as

2 **step** 1 **until** − 6

the statement after **do** is never executed.

In a case such as

for a : = 1 **step** 1 **until** a

the statement is obeyed an infinite number of times and the program enters an endless loop.

Care must be taken when dealing with real quantities in a **step–until** type of **for** statement. In a statement like

for a : = 1 **step** .1 **until** 11.5

there is a danger that, owing to the representation of real numbers, continued addition of .1 to 1 may result in a number slightly in excess of 11.5. In that case, the last iteration would not be performed. The statement is better written as

for a : = 1 **step** .1 **until** 11.51

In all three types of **for** statement the controlled variable is 'undefined' (left to the discretion of the compiler-writer!) when the loop has been executed for all values in the list. In the example above, a should not be used outside the range of the **for** statement until the programmer has assigned it a value.

Single expression type

A succession of arithmetic expressions separated by commas forms the simplest type of **for** list, e.g.

for a : = 3, 7, 13, 5, 67, 31 **do** print(ln(a), 2, 4);

would execute the print statement for the values of a in the list. An example with expressions would be

for a : = d/e, f * g, sqrt(h − k − v) **do** print(ln(a), 2, 4);

While *elements*

It is often desired to perform a loop until some function of the controlled variable goes outside certain bounds. This can be done with the third type of **for** list element which has the general form

arithmetic expression **while** Boolean expression

This sets the value of the controlled variable to the arithmetic expression and performs the range only if the Boolean expression is true. As soon as the Boolean expression is false, the program continues with the statement after the **for** statement. A typical example would be

> **for** a : = a + 1 **while** term − oldterm > $_{10}$ − 7 **do**
>   **begin**
>   oldterm : = term; term : = term + 1/a
>   **end**;

In the above example the expression term − oldterm must be given an initial value > $_{10}$ − 7 otherwise the range will not be executed at all.

General notes on all types of list element

All types of list element may appear in a **for** statement; for example,

> **for** n : = 1, 7 **step** 2 **until** 19, n + 2, 25 **step** 3 **until** 34

denotes the sequence 1, 7, 9, 11, 13, 15, 17, 19, 23, 25, 28, 31, 34. Notice that n + 2 after the first **step–until** element assumes n has the value of the first item in the **step–until** element for which the range was not executed.

It is usual to assign an initial value to the controlled variable when a **while** element is used. The example used to show the use of the **while** element could be written as

> **for** a : = 1, a + 1 **while** term–oldterm > $_{10}$ − 7 **do**
>   **begin**
>   oldterm : = term; term : = term + 1/a
>   **end**;

A **for** statement is not classed as an unconditional statement. It may appear after **then** in an **if–then** statement but not following **then** in an **if–then–else** statement otherwise ambiguity occurs. The permissible forms are:

> **if** n ≠ 0 **then for** a : = 1 **step** 1 **until** 5 **do** S1
> **if** n ≠ 0 **then begin**
>   **for** a : = 1 **step** 1 **until** 5 **do** S1 **end else** S2

where S1 and S2 are any statements.

for statements can be nested so that one **for** statement controls another **for** statement. In the following example it is desired to use the formula x = a/b to tabulate values of x for all combinations of a and b in the ranges 100 ⩽ a ⩽ 500 and 1 ⩽ b ⩽ 10. a is to be increased in steps of 10 and b in steps of 1. A section of program to accomplish this is given below.

> **for** a : = 100 **step** 10 **until** 500 **do**
> **for** b : = 1 **step** 1 **until** 10 **do**
>   **begin**
>   x : = a/b; print(a, 3, 0); print(b, 2, 0);
>   print(x, 3, 3); newline(1)
>   **end**;

4

A **for** statement may be labelled, for example,

start; **for** 1 : = 1 **step** 1 **until** 100 **do** S;

(S is any statement.)

Exits from the range of the **for** statement by means of a **goto** statement are allowed, and the controlled variable keeps its current value on exit. A **goto** statement outside the range of a **for** statement may not refer to a label within the range of the **for** statement. Such a jump would bypass the setting of the controlled variable. Sometimes it is desired to bypass part of the body of a **for** statement and go to the beginning for the next performance of the range. In that case a label has to be put at the end of the range. (To jump to a label before the word **for** would put the controlled variable back to the initial condition.)

Since only a statement can be labelled, it is apparently not possible to jump to **end**. However, this difficulty may be solved by permitting a *dummy statement*, which is an empty space that does nothing, for example,

newline(1); **end**;

This is a dummy statement after the newline instruction.

In the following example, the square roots of ten numbers read from paper tape are to be printed with the natural exception of any zero or negative items on the tape. It illustrates the use of a labelled dummy statement at the end of the range of a **for** statement.

```
for n : = 1 step 1 until 10 do
    begin
        a : = read; if a ≤ 0 then goto repeat;
        print(sqrt(a), 4, 4); newline(1);
    repeat : end;
```

(This example using **else** could be done without the **goto** statement.)

Arrays (subscripted variables)

A programmer often needs to perform operations upon tables, matrices and similar groups of like variables. Each member of the set or group can be referred to by a distinct variable name, but it is better to deal with the whole set as an *array*.

An identifier of the normal type is used to name the whole array, and this name, followed by one or more subscripts, refers to a particular element. A subscripted variable can appear in a program wherever an ordinary variable is permitted.

Any reference to a subscripted variable must be preceded by the appropriate type declaration for an array. The most usual forms are mentioned below:

real array A[1: 10], k[0: 9];

The **real** could be omitted before **array**. Two arrays are declared here; both are vectors with ten elements. The former has **bounds** from 1 to 10 and the latter from 0 to 9. If it is vital to the program, negative bounds can be used; a vector with ten elements could be declared as

X[−2: 7]

There is no limit in Algol to the number of dimensions an array can possess. Individual bound pairs are separated by commas, so a two-dimensional array would be declared as

B[1: 5, 1: 10]

The above array, B, has five rows and ten columns.

In the program, an array item is referred to by its identifier and its appropriate number of subscripts, for example,

A[7]:=e;
B[2, 4]:=h;

(this is the fourth column on the second row).

Subscripts can be arithmetic expressions although it generally is time-wasting to use anything more complicated than an add or substract when evaluating subscripts. If a subscript has a **real** value it is rounded to the nearest integer. Examples of array items with expressions as subscripts are

X[n]   k[j−t]   B[1+m, entier(q+4)]

An array having **integer** elements has the type declaration as

integer array

The word **integer** here is *never* omitted.

Several arrays of identical type and bounds may be declared at once with the identifiers separated by commas, for example,

integer array A, C, D[1: 100];

declares three integer arrays of 100 elements.

In multiple assignment statements the subscripts are evaluated first in sequence from left to right and the value of the right-hand expression is assigned to left-hand variables. In the sequence of instructions:

k:=1; A[k]:=k:=5;

A[1] will be set to 5.

An example of the use of arrays is the following section of program, which reads and stores 100 numbers from paper tape as well as calculating their sum prior to some statistical calculations:

```
total:=0; for n:=1 step 1 until 100 do
   begin A[n]:=read; total:=total+A[n]
   end;
```

Exercises 4.2

Do questions 1–7 of Exercises 4.1 using **for** statements.

Comment

Judicious use of the **comment** facility can help to make a program clearer to other users. Comments are ignored by the compiler. Any sequence of basic symbols can be used for comment if they are introduced in one of the following ways.

1. Introduced by **comment** following either a semi-colon or **begin**. Succeeding symbols *up to* the next semi-colon are treated as comment and ignored by the compiler, e.g.

   begin comment this calculates the mean;

2. Any symbols after **end** up to a semi-colon, **end** or **else** are treated as comment, for example,

   end of mean calculation;

Below is a simple program with comments.

```
begin comment program to show the use of comment;
real x, t; integer n; comment start of program;
t:=0; for n:=1 step 1 until 10 do
   begin comment start of reading loop;
        x:=read; t:=t+x
   end of loop;
print(t/10, 4, 4)
end
```

Without comment the program reads:

```
begin real x, t; integer n;
t:=0; for n:=1 step 1 until 10 do
   begin x:=read; t:=t+x
   end; print(t/10, 4, 4)
end
```

Block structure

A block is a compound statement with at least one type declaration after **begin**, for example,

    begin real x; x: = read **end**;

is a block. All the examples given so far have been of programs containing one block.

A block is defined as an unconditional statement so that it can be used within **for** statements and both types of conditional statements.

A program can have a complicated structure of blocks within blocks but a beginner often restricts a program to a single block even though the facility of using more than one block is an important feature of Algol. The only case in elementary Algol programming where a single block program will not suffice is when a dynamic array (discussed later in this section) is used. The use of more than one block entails certain problems with regard to the use of identifiers, which will now be discussed. If a program has more than one block it must consist of one all-embracing outermost block containing any number of inner blocks. A typical skeleton structure of such a program would be:

    begin real x, y;
      L:
            begin integer q, r:
            M;
            end;
            begin real i, j;
            N:
            end;
      P:
    end

An identifier at the head of a block or appearing as a label in that block is available for use in that block and in any blocks enclosed within it. In the example above, the variables x, y and the labels P, N can be referred to by the two inner blocks. An identifier is often said to be *global* to enclosed blocks and *local* to the block in which it is declared.

No variable or label in any of the inner blocks can be referred to by the outer block or by the other inner block. Identifiers local to a block can only be referred to in the same block or in blocks inner to it.

It follows therefore that entry to a block can only be through the **begin** symbol of the block; otherwise the declarations are bypassed. The range in which identifiers have validity is sometimes called the scope of the identifier. It is possible to jump out of an inner block by a **goto** to a label outside it, but it is not possible to go from an outer block to an inner block except to a label before the **begin** of the inner block.

If the same name is used for an identifier in both an inner and outer block any reference to that identifier in the inner block refers to the inner block declaration and 'masks out' the outer block declaration, for example,

```
begin real x, y;
  N:
    begin real c, x;
    N:
    end
end
```

In the above structure any reference to the variable x or the label N in the inner block refers to those in the inner block.

When an inner block is left, the value of any variable declared in that block is lost and the compiler uses its store location for other purposes.

This loss of value can be avoided if a type declaration is prefixed by **own**, for example,

```
own integer n, m;
own real h, x, y;
own array A[1: 100];
```

In this case, a variable on re-entry to a block has the value it possessed when the last exit from the block was made. The variable is *not* accessible outside the scope of the block.

One of the chief uses of block structure (and the only one for the average beginner) is for dynamic arrays. These are arrays in which the bounds are declared in terms of variables not constants, e.g.

```
integer array I[1: m];
```

The variables used to denote bounds must be declared and have a value assigned in a block outer to the array declaration.

In the following section of program a tape is punched with a number which indicates the number of items following for which the arithmetic mean is to be printed, and the numbers stored.

```
begin integer number;
number: = read;
  begin real total, x, y; integer m, n; array X[1: number];
  total: = 0; for m: = 1 step 1 until number do
      begin X[m]: = read; total: = total + X[m]
      end;
    print(total/number, 4, 4)
        (here continues the rest of the program)
  end
end
```

This is probably the chief use of block structure. Another use is when a large program is divided up between several programmers. Each one writes a block, and it does not matter if more than one use identical identifier names as they are local to their particular block. Naturally the outermost block must contain variable declarations for communication between the various inner blocks.

Yet another use is for two large arrays to be declared in parallel inner blocks if they are never needed at the same time. In this way they share the same computer storage space.

It must be observed that compilers do not allow the facility of declaring dynamic own arrays.

Exercises 4.3

1. Read ten numbers, compute and print the average, and print the number with the greatest absolute deviation from the average.
2. Write a sequence of instructions to divide each element of a matrix with five rows and three columns by the largest element.
3. Write a section of program to print out the largest element of a matrix with three rows and four columns. It is also desired to print out the row and column of the largest element.
4. Print the prime numbers between 3 and 100.
5. Print a square with 19 rows and 19 columns with each of the rows and columns containing once only each of the numbers 1–19 (Latin square).

Procedures

It is often desired to use common sequences of instructions at various points in the program. This idea was mentioned in chapter 2, where it was referred to as a subroutine.

In Algol, subroutines are called *procedures*. The sequence of instructions is written at the head of the block in which we wish to make use of the procedure. The actual instructions in the procedure are known as the procedure *body*.

The procedure is *not*, however, obeyed at the head of the block. The instructions are only entered when the procedure name or identifier is written in the program proper. This reference to the procedure identifier is known as the *call* of that procedure. A procedure can be a simple statement, compound statement or block. An example of the simplest kind of procedure, a single statement, is given below with a section of program showing the calls.

```
begin real x, y, z;
procedure tan; x := sin(y)/cos(y);
y := read; tan; print(x, 2, 4); newline(1);
z := read; ...
    y := z; tan; print(x, 2, 4); ...
end
```

Here the statement in the procedure tan is only obeyed when the identifier tan is written in the program proper.

A procedure in the form of a single statement is rare. Below is a more realistic procedure in the form of a compound statement.

procedure hypotenuse;
begin h:=sqrt(S1 ↑ 2+S2 ↑ 2); print(S1, 3, 3); print(S2, 3, 3);
    print(h, 3, 3); newline(1)
end;

The above procedure is of limited value insofar as it is using global variables. It always expects the sides to be in the variables S1 and S2 and always puts the results in the variable h. To convert sides, it would be necessary to first put them in the variables S1 and S2.

Global variables are not normally employed as arguments for a procedure. A procedure usually has its own arguments which are called *formal parameters*. These can be replaced by any arithmetic expression in the procedure call. In this way the procedure hypotenuse could be

procedure hypotenuse(x, y, z); **real** x, y, z;
begin x = sqrt(y ↑ 2+z ↑ 2); print(y, 3, 3); print(z, 3, 3);
    print(x, 3, 3); newline(1)
end;

and a typical call replacing the formal parameters by actual parameters could be

    hypotenuse (e, f, g);

In this example any arithmetic operation performed on the formal parameter y would in practice be performed on f. The definition of a procedure at the head of a block is known as the *declaration* of the procedure. After the word **procedure** and the identifier of the procedure, the formal parameters (if any) are listed in parentheses. The formal parameters are usually separated by commas as in the above example.

There must be the same number of actual parameters in a procedure call as there are formal parameters in the declaration.

The simple replacement of the formal parameters by the corresponding actual parameters is referred to as *call by name*. The formal parameters are dummies, and no values are assigned to them. All the parameters in the above example are 'called by name'. If the actual parameter was an expression such as b ↑ 2−4 ∗ a ∗ c, the expression would have to be evaluated afresh each time the formal parameter was mentioned in the procedure. This would be wasteful and so for parameters which input an argument to a procedure there is a superior technique known as *call by value*. This involves having a special type declaration **value** (only usable in a procedure) for such parameters. In the above procedure, hypotenuse, it would be appropriate to give y and z a **value** declaration, but x should not be treated in this manner as it merely transmits a result to the corresponding actual parameter that could never be an arithmetic expression.

A special storage location is created for each formal parameter of **value** type, and its value is calculated at the start of each call of the procedure and stored in this location so that much time is saved if the actual parameter is an expression.

value type would not be suitable for formal parameters where it is desired to store the result of the calculation. Here it is wanted to transfer the result to the actual parameter in the program proper.

Below is hypotenuse rewritten with a value call.

> **procedure** hypotenuse (x, y, z); **value** y, z;
> **real** x, y, z;
> **begin** x : = sqrt(y ↑ 2 + z ↑ 2); print(y, 3, 3); print(z, 3, 3);
>   print(x, 3, 3); newline(1);
> **end**

It will be observed that type **value** is *always* declared first and that variables of type **value** are always redeclared; usually as **integer** or **real**.

Many procedures deal with arrays. The array declaration as a formal parameter has no bounds. The bounds of the equivalent actual parameter are substituted but any reference to any array item in the procedure body must have the appropriate number of subscripts. If any array is called by value, then an equivalent array to the actual parameter is created in the computer storage for use only within the procedure.

The following procedure calculates the mean of an array given upper and lower bounds and will illustrate the treatment of an array in a procedure.

> **procedure** mean(X, m, n, a); **value** m, n; **array** X; **real** a;
>   **integer** m, n;
> **begin real** total; **integer** count;
>   total : = 0; **for** count : = m **step** 1 **until** n **do**
>   total : = total + X[count];
>   a : = total/(n − m + 1)
> **end**;

A typical call would be mean (A, 1, 40, b). This would store the average of the first 40 elements of the array A in b.

There is a type declaration **label** which is only used inside procedures. This is a formal parameter for which the actual parameter is a label inside the program proper so that an exit jump (often inserted to deal with validity failure of the input) can be made to various labels in the main program.

A procedure with a **label** declaration could have the heading

compute(a, b, L); **value** a; **real** a, b; **label** L;

Typical calls would be

compute(x, y, finish);
compute(i, r, return);

finish and return would be labels in the block where the procedure was called or in a block outer to the call.

Functions

If we wish to use a procedure that forms a single result, a form defining a function is often used. This form can be used as part of an arithmetic expression and is not a complete statement in its call like the procedures encountered in the previous section.

This type of procedure has a type symbol before **procedure** so typical functions begin with

real procedure
integer procedure

The desired single result is placed in the procedure name.
Below are examples of functions.

real procedure square(a, b); **value** a, b; **real** a, b;
square: $=(a+b) \uparrow 2$;

integer procedure mean(A, m, n); **value** m, n; **integer** m, n;
integer array A;
begin integer total, count;
total: $=0$; **for** count: $=m$ **step** 1 **until** n **do**
total: $=$ total $+$ A[count];
mean: $=$ total $\div (n-m+1)$;

Typical calls would be
k: $=$ square(j, q);
r: $=$ x $+$ square(y, z) -6;
1: $=$ d $+$ g $-$ mean(items, 1, 30);
z: $=$ e*sqrt(mean(X, 1, 25) $+$ p);

All the type declarations such as **label** and **value** which are available to a **procedure** (see above) are also available to a function.

If a function is written with the same identifier as one of the standard functions, such as sin, the standard function is masked out for the scope of the programmer's own function.

Recursion

An Algol procedure may refer to itself within its own procedure body. Such a procedure is called a *recursive* procedure. The usual example is given below; a **for** statement would be more efficient.

integer procedure factorial(n); **value**(n); **integer**(n);
if n = 1 **then** factorial := 1
    else factorial := n * factorial (n − 1);
If 4 replaces n at the call
  then factorial := 4 * factorial(3)
$$\equiv 4 * 3 \times \text{factorial}(2)$$
$$\equiv 4 * 3 * 2 * \text{factorial}(1)$$
$$\equiv 4 * 3 * 2 * 1$$

To evaluate n!, n procedure calls are required.

This is a very elegant method of programming which appeals to a certain type of mind, but it is hardly the most efficient and should rarely if ever be used by beginners. Any **for** statement can be expressed as a recursive procedure but the **for** statement has far greater efficiency.

Certain advanced types of symbol manipulation can be accomplished only by the use of recursive procedures. Recursion is used most in the construction of compilers and in linguistic data processing.

Conditional arithmetic expressions

An alternative way of writing

if n = 5 **then** m := 1 **else** m := 0;

would be

m := **if** n = 5 **then** 1 **else** 0;

The above form is a conditional arithmetic expression.

There is no form of conditional arithmetic expression which corresponds to the **if–then** form of conditional statement; an expression such as

m := **if** n = 5 **then** 1;

would be meaningless as no provision is made to give m a value if n ≠ 5.

then in a conditional arithmetic expression can only be followed by an unconditional arithmetic expression; that is to say, **then if** is not permitted. This restriction can be overcome by the use of parentheses, for example,

k := **if** x = 9 **then** (**if** y = 7 **then** 2 **else** 1) **else** 3;

Some very complicated expressions of the above type are possible and generally should be avoided in the interests of easy readability of the program.

A conditional arithmetic expression can follow an arithmetic operator from which it must be separated by parentheses, for example,

b : = a + (**if** n = 2 **then** e **else** h) − sqrt(d);

Switches and designational expressions

Sometimes it is desired to jump from one point in a program to several others depending on the value of a particular variable. It is possible to do this by a series of conditional statements. This can be effected in a simpler way by making use of a *switch designator* instead of a label in a **goto** statement, for example,

goto return[n];

The switch declaration appears at the head of the block in which it is desired to be used. It consists of a series of labels, for example,

switch return : = L, out,finish,again,out;

Then in the above example, if n were 1 the program would jump to the label L, 2 to out, 3 to finish, 4 to again and 5 to out.

The contents of the square brackets after the switch name can be an arithmetic expression but it must never be less than unity or greater than the number of labels in the declaration of the switch.

The following small example shows the use of a switch. It is desired to print the day on which January 1 falls in 1966, 1967 and 1968 given that 1 January 1965 was a Friday.

```
begin integer year; switch P: = Q, R, S;
for year: = 1966 step 1 until 1968 do
    begin goto P[year − 1965]; T: newline(1) end;
goto out;
Q: writetext ({SATURDAY}); goto T;
R: writetext ({SUNDAY});   goto T;
S: writetext ({MONDAY});   goto T;
out: end
```

A switch is the second form of a simple designational expression, the first being a simple label after the **goto**.

A conditional designational expression is analogous to a conditional arithmetic expression mentioned previously. Typical examples would be

goto if n = m **then** return **else** finish;
goto if a > b **then** branch[j]**else** L;

Boolean operations

So far only certain types of Boolean expressions in conditional statements have been considered. Algol is rich in facilities for conducting Boolean operations in which the interest is on whether a value is true or false and not in any numerical quantity. The beginner is unlikely to need great acquaintance with the Boolean facilities unless he is concerned with circuit design or symbolic logic, so we will not go into great detail.

Boolean variables can be simple variables or members of an array. Examples of their type declaration are

Boolean p, q, r; **Boolean array** X[1 : 20];

Algol provides five Boolean operators of which two have already been encountered.

¬ not   ¬ A is false if A is true and vice versa.
∧ and   A ∧ B is true if both A and B are true; otherwise false.
∨ or   A ∨ B is true if either A or B is true.
⊃ implies   A ⊃ B is true if A is false or B is true; otherwise false.
≡ equivalent A ≡ B is true if A and B have the same truth values; otherwise false.

Boolean variables can be combined using the above operators to form Boolean expressions, for example, n ∨ m.

A value can be inserted in a Boolean variable in the following ways:
1. Using **true** or **false**. u : = **true**; v : = **false**
2. Using a Boolean expression;

    n : = k = 4;
    n : = A > B;
    n : = D; (D is a Boolean variable.)

3. There is a Boolean procedure analogous to real and integer procedures and these can give a truth value to a Boolean variable, for example,

    B : = truth(A, m, n);

where truth is a Boolean procedure.

Highly elaborate Boolean expressions are not likely to be used by beginners. The rules for the evaluation of a Boolean expression are:
1. Arithmetic expressions are evaluated first.
2. The truth values of relations are determined.
3. Boolean operations are performed in the order: not, and, or, implies, equivalent.

There is a conditional form of the Boolean expression like the conditional arithmetic expression† but it is rarely necessary.

The most common use of Boolean variables is in programs concerned with logical operations. They have a definite use, however, in numerical programs when they can prevent the frequent evaluation of an arithmetic

† See Section 3,4.2 of the Algol Report, *Communications of the Association for Computing Machinery*, January 1963, pp. 1–17.

expression for purposes of comparison and thus time can be saved. For example, if it is desired to test many times in a program the relation

$$b * b > 4 * a * c$$

the truth value of it can be assigned to a Boolean variable and subsequent tests can be made with this Boolean variable:

B:=b * b>4 * a * c;
if B then...

It will be observed that the form **if B** is used and not **if B≡true**.

5
FORTRAN

Fortran is the most widely used of the high-level programming languages. It is primarily a language for scientific and mathematical work, yet before the development of Cobol it was used successfully for some business data-processing applications as it is more useful for commercial applications than Algol.

Fortran is short for *For*mula *tra*nslation and was produced by IBM for their 704 computer in 1957†. A new version of Fortran, known as Fortran II, became available in 1958 and a more powerful variety, known as Fortran IV, appeared in 1962. A version of Fortran is provided for the majority of computers found in Britain. There are many different versions of Fortran and the user cannot be too emphatically advised to consult the Fortran programming manual of the appropriate computer for full details of the particular dialect for that computer.

An attempt was made in 1966 to define the Fortran language. The American Standards Association Document (X3.9.1966) defines Basic Fortran (resembling Fortran II), and another (X3.10.1966) defines A.S.A. Fortran (resembling Fortran IV). 'A Study of Fortran Compatibility' by C. F. Schofield (University of London Atlas Computing Service 1968) is a guide to some of the variations in some common Fortran dialects.

This chapter demonstrates the features of Basic Fortran that are common to most compilers and are capable of being used on small computers. The final section in the chapter describes some features of A.S.A. Fortran that have been implemented on some larger computers. There is a larger body of fully tested and proved programs written in Fortran than any other language; a typical example is the comprehensive BMD series of bio-medical statistical programs of the University of California. The popularity of the language is reflected in the distribution of over 228,000 programming manuals by 1963.

Layout of a Fortran program

The statements of a Fortran program are usually punched on cards in the following format. Statements are normally one per card. The meaning of the terms used will become clear in the course of this chapter. Each line would be punched on a separate card.

1. Columns 1–5 contain a statement number. Blanks and leading zeros are ignored.

† A brief history of Fortran appeared in the March 1963 issue of the *Communications of the Association for Computing Machinery.*

2. Column 6 is blank for the first card of a statement; for subsequent cards it contains by convention the number of that card in the statement.
3. Columns 7–72 contain the Fortran statement. Blanks are ignored except in certain places that will be indicated later in this chapter.
4. A letter C in column 1 means that this card is a comment, and columns 2–72 may be used for the comment.
5. Columns 73–80 are ignored by the compiler and may be used for identification.

The number of continuation cards permitted varies from one compiler to another.

Various formats of Fortran for paper tape are in existence. The reader is referred to the appropriate Fortran manual for details.

Variables

The term *variable* is used for a part of the computer store that holds a numerical quantity in the course of the program. Variable names must start with a letter and can only contain letters and digits, for example

ITEM   TYPE2   X007   CORINNE   GILLIAN

The length of a variable name varies with the different implementations of the language.

Variables can hold either real (floating-point) numbers or integers. A real variable begins with a letter A–H or O–Z; an integer variable begins with a letter I–N.

Thus DELTA and EPSILON will hold real quantities whilst KAPPA and LAMBDA will hold integers. If it is desired that a name beginning with a 'real' letter (such as TAX) should hold an integer, then it can be prefaced with an 'integer' letter, e.g. ITAX.

Variable names can be considered (by beginners) as being unique within a program. The range of integers and real numbers that can be represented varies from computer to computer and will be given in the particular Fortran manual.

Constants

It is sometimes necessary to insert a definite numerical value in a variable. The form of the number that is inserted is known as a *constant*. There is a sharp distinction in Fortran between real and integer constants.

Integer constants

These are whole numbers, assumed positive if they are unsigned and written without a decimal point. The presence or absence of a decimal point is the distinction between real and integer constants. Acceptable integer constants would be:

$$10 \qquad 0$$
$$-457 \qquad +295$$

Real constants

(*a*) Without an exponent.

Real constants without an exponent are the most common and consist of a number with a decimal point; they are assumed positive if unsigned. Typical ones would be:

$$-1.234 \qquad 0.987$$
$$98.06 \qquad 0.235$$
$$76. \qquad 0.0$$

The reasons for such apparent oddities as 0.0 and 76. will be explained in the next section.

(*b*) With an exponent.

It is possible to follow a real constant by the letter E and a one- or two-digit integer, which may be signed and which represents the power of 10 by which the number preceding E is to be multiplied. This forms a convenient way of representing very large and very small numbers without recourse to writing strings of zeros.

$$3.0E+6 = 3 \times 10^6 \qquad = 3{,}000{,}000$$
$$-5.E-4 \; = -5 \times 10^{-4} = -.0005$$
$$7.14E9 \; = 7.14 \times 10^9 = 7{,}140{,}000{,}000$$
$$-.2E5 \quad = -.2 \times 10^5 \; = -20{,}000$$

Arithmetic statements

The simplest forms of a Fortran arithmetic statement are:

$$N = M$$

and

$$K = 9$$

Some compilers will allow a mixture of integers and real numbers in an arithmetic statement, but as a general rule types should not be mixed because, if the program is to be run on different computers, a compiler will almost invariably be encountered that will not accept them. Therefore, expressions like

$$A = 10$$
$$K = 4.0$$
$$U = J$$

should *not* be written.

The next section will illustrate a method of storing the contents of a real variable in an integer variable and vice versa. The first two of the three previous expressions above should be rewritten as:

A = 10.
K = 4

The effect of the arithmetic statement is to set the variable at the left-hand side of = equal to the right-hand expression (in the above two examples, a single constant). No variable at the right-hand side is changed by being used to compute a value to insert in the left-hand variable. The right-hand side is often known as an arithmetic expression.

There are five basic arithmetic operations represented by five distinct symbols:

Addition   +
Subtraction   −
Multiplication   *
Exponentiation   **
Division   /

The combination ** is considered to be one symbol. It is illegal to write two operators together so there is no confusion between * and **. Examples of statements with arithmetic expressions in the right-hand parts are:

K = L
A = B − V
ITEM = IPRICE * IVAL
AVE = SUM/TOTAL
LPOWER = L ** N
MEAN = (I + L) * (J − N)

The chief rules for the writing of arithmetic expressions are:

1. Parentheses may be used as in ordinary mathematical notation.
2. Any expression, whether real or integer, may have a positive or negative integer quantity following ** (e.g. A ** 3). However, only real expressions may be raised to a fractional power (e.g. A ** 2.4).
3. Two operators must not appear together; so A * − B is incorrect and must be rewritten as A * (− B).
4. When parentheses do not specify the hierarchy of operations in an expression the following order prevails: All exponentiation is done first, then multiplications and divisions followed by addition and subtraction.

5. Within a sequence of consecutive multiplications and/or divisions or additions and/or subtractions, the operations are performed from left to right unless otherwise specified by parentheses. Thus

$$E/F * U \quad \text{would mean} \quad \frac{E}{F}.U$$

and

$$L - M + N \quad \text{would mean} \quad (L - M) + N$$

6. Multiplication is *never* implicit. A * Y is correct: *not* AY. The full meaning of = in Fortran is brought out in the statement

$$N = N + 1$$

Algebraically this is nonsense, yet in programming it is a perfectly valid and very common and useful type of statement. It means that 1 is added to N and the result stored away in N. It is commonly used in loops when augmenting counts.

The result of an integer division is truncated to the whole number nearest zero, i.e. the fractional part is discarded so that in the following sequence of statements

$$N = 2$$
$$J = 3$$
$$K = N/J$$

K would have the value 0.

Sometimes the effect of a truncation like the above is forgotten and gives rise to unexpected results.

A statement can have a *statement number* punched in columns 1–5 of the card. Leading zeros should not be punched. Statement numbers can be given in any order in the program. Only certain statements need have numbers; this will become clear in subsequent sections.

Standard functions

The power of a Fortran arithmetic statement can be enhanced by the use of the standard functions provided by the compiler. The provision of functions varies from one compiler to another. The list below gives the functions that are invariably supplied. All work on real arguments except for FLOATF. The argument of any can be an arithmetic expression; the argument in the following list is denoted by X.

ABSF(X)	absolute value
ATANF(X)	inverse tangent; result in radians between $-\pi/2$ and $\pi/2$
COSF(X)	argument in radians
SINF(X)	argument in radians

TANF(X)   argument in radians
EXPF(X)   exponential
FLOATF(X)   converts an integer to real number
LOGF(X)   natural logarithm
SQRTF(X)   square root

The following function has a real argument and gives an integer result:

INTF(X)   largest integer $\leqslant$ X

The appropriate Fortran programming manual should be consulted for details of particular functions available on an individual computer. The argument of a standard function should always be enclosed in parentheses, for example

$$X = SQRTF(B ** 2 - 4 * A * C)$$

Uses of the functions FLOATF and INTF can enable real and integer variables to be mixed in an arithmetic statement, for example,

$$Y = D + FLOATF(J)$$
$$K = I - INTF(H)$$

In some versions a function can be the argument of another function so that expressions like LOGF(ABSF(Y)) are possible.

Simple input and output

Data for a Fortran program are usually read from punched cards. There is no standard version of paper-tape input; for this facility the reader is referred to the appropriate programming manual.

A type READ instruction would be:

READ 4, I, J
4 FORMAT (I6, I4)

This means that two numbers would be read from a punched card into the integer variables I and J according to the data layout of the punched card described in the FORMAT statement.

In this case the first six columns of the card would be read into I and the next four into J. If the card was punched:

xxxxxxxxxx
67 238

I would contain 67 and J 238, The rest of the card could *not* be read by any subsequent READ statement as a READ statement reads at least one card at a time. The FORMAT statement can appear anywhere in the program; it is often customary to insert it immediately after the input or output statement to which it refers.

The I in the FORMAT statement refers to the mode in which the card is to be read: I means integer mode. The form of this mode is

In .

where n refers to the number of columns on the punched card (or *field width*) that it is desired to read into each variable.

Leading blanks (as in the above example) are ignored, but a blank in the middle of a number on the card will cause trouble. If signs are punched they must be counted in the field width.

The form of the READ statement is

READ n, *list*

where n is the number of the FORMAT statement describing card layout. Each item in the list is matched with the appropriate layout description in the FORMAT statement scanned from left to right.

It is common for number fields on a punched card to be separated by blank columns. The FORMAT specification

nX

where n is an integer, enables blank columns to be skipped by the READ statement. In some versions of Fortran the X need not be separated from the next specification on the FORMAT list by a comma. The sequence of statements

READ 6, I, J, K, L
6   FORMAT(I5, 5X, I4, 6X, I5, 5X, I6)

would read columns 1–5 to I, 11–14 to J, 21–25 to K and 31–36 to L. Columns 6–10, 15–20, 26–30 would be dealt with by the X specifications in the FORMAT statement and would be assumed to be blank.

The X specification naturally corresponds to no variable in the list in the READ statement. Since leading blanks are ignored, the above example could have the FORMAT statement

(I5, I9, I11, I11)

Often certain fields are repeated on the card layout as in the following example:

READ 4, L, M, N
4   FORMAT(3(I7, 3X))

If any number of specifications are repeated they are enclosed in parentheses preceded by a number giving the required number of repetitions as in the above example. A single specification can be repeated in a similar manner by writing in front of the specification a number showing the number of fields involved. For example,

   3I5

is the same as

   I5, I5, I5

The most usual way of reading real numbers from a punched card is to use the F FORMAT specification. The form is

   Fm.n

where m and n are integers, m representing the field width or number of columns and n the number of fractional digits.

If a card was punched

   7327   − 123456

the statements

```
      READ 9, A, B
   9  FORMAT(F4.2, 3X, F7.4)
```

would put 73.27 in A and − 12.3456 in B.

If a decimal point is punched on the card, it overrides the number of decimal places requested in the second part of the F specification.

If the first ten columns of a card were punched

   1234.56789

the sequence of statements

```
      READ 21, G
   21 FORMAT(F10.6)
```

would store 1234.56789 in G. The punched decimal point overrides the six decimal places of the FORMAT statement.

The above specifications are also used when printing results.

The statement for printing is

   PRINT format statement number, list

It must be remembered to allow a space for a negative sign in the FORMAT specification. A typical sequence of instructions for printing would be

```
      PRINT 2, W, K, T, N
   2  FORMAT(F6.3, 4X, I5, 5X, F7.2, 3X, I4)
```

The line of print could appear as:

   − 7.245   363   386.19   8752

If it is necessary to use a print statement to print on more than one line a slash / must be used in the FORMAT statement to terminate a line. If I = 4, J = 6 and K = 16 the following statements

        PRINT 12, I, J, K
    12 FORMAT(2(I3, 2X)/I3)

would print

    4 6
    17

The inclusion of // in a FORMAT statement produces a blank line before the next printed line so that the statements

        PRINT 23, I, J, K
    23 FORMAT(2(I3, 2X)//I3)

with the above values in I, J and K would print

    4 6

    17

n slashes will produce n−1 blank lines.
It must be emphasized that / cannot be preceded by an integer. 3/ is incorrect and must be written as ///.
A slash in an input FORMAT statement causes a new card to be read; n slashes will skip n−1 cards. The following statements would read two numbers where each number is punched in the first four columns of a separate card.

        READ 192, I, J
    192 FORMAT(I4/I4)

Each PRINT statement prints at least a line. This is analogous to the READ statement reading at least one card. It is never possible to print on the same line with two different PRINT statements. If it is desired to punch cards instead of print results on a line printer, there is a PUNCH statement that is in form completely like the PRINT statement. If it is desired to print or punch text, the H FORMAT specification is used.
The form is

    nH

where the n characters following the H are output. This is the only case where a blank in a Fortran statement is not ignored. A blank occurring between the H and the next field specification is counted in the number of characters.

In some versions of Fortran, the first character after the H is a carriage-control character; blank causes a single space, 0 a double space and 1 a new page. The appropriate programming manual should be consulted for the exact details of this facility. The statements

        PRINT 8, X, L
     8 FORMAT(3HX = F8.3, 10X, 3HL = I6)

could print

        X = -212.456   L = 976537

It will be observed that a comma is not needed to separate an H specification from the next specification. A PRINT statement which consists only of H specifications (or X and H specifications) needs no list, for example,

        PRINT 45
     45 FORMAT(14HSALES ANALYSIS)

Transfer of control

It is sometimes necessary to cease obeying Fortran statements one after the other and to skip forwards or backwards over some statements to another point in the program. This can be done by the use of a GO TO statement. This is followed by a statement number, e.g. GO TO 76. The program will then proceed to obey the statement numbered 76 and will proceed in sequence from that point.

One of the most important facilities of a digital computer is the power to transfer control to various parts of the program according to a decision taken by the computer. These were the steps which, in chapter 2, were written in a flowchart in a diamond-shaped 'box'. In Fortran, the IF statement provides this facility. The form is:

        IF (e) S1, S2, S3

where e is any arithmetic expression and S1, S2 and S3 are statement numbers. If the expression is negative, program control is transferred to the first statement, it if is zero to the second and if it is positive to the third.

The following simple example demonstrates the working of the IF statement. A number is read from a card and we wish to print the square of the number if it is positive and the number itself if it is negative. If it is zero, the word ZERO should be printed.

```
    READ 1, A
1   FORMAT(F8.3)
    IF(A) 2, 3, 4
2   PRINT 1, A
5   STOP
4   B = A * A
    PRINT 6, B
6   FORMAT(F13.3)
    GO TO 5
3   PRINT 7
7   FORMAT(4HZERO)
    GO TO 5
```

It will be seen that there is a statement STOP, which marks a point in the program where we wish to cease computing. There can be numerous STOP statements in the program; two more could have been used in the previous example instead of GO TO 5.

After a STOP statement the computation cannot be easily resumed. If we need to effect some operator intervention (e.g. to insert a new deck of cards in the reader), the PAUSE statement is used, which allows a button to be pressed on the console to resume computing after the appropriate operator action has been taken.

The END statement is a signal to the *compiler* that the end of the program has been reached in programs like the preceding example. The END statement in larger programs is discussed in greater detail later in this chapter. For the moment it can be assumed that this must be the last statement in any program.

A complete program will now be given to read ten numbers from ten punched cards and to print their average. It will make use of the looping technique mentioned in chapter 2.

```
    N = 0
    TOTAL = 0.
1   READ 2, A
2   FORMAT(F5.2)
    TOTAL = TOTAL + A
    N = N + 1
    IF (N - 10) 1, 3, 3
3   AVE = TOTAL/10.
    PRINT 2, AVE
    STOP
    END
```

It will be noticed that the same FORMAT statement can be used for both reading and printing if suitable and that the same statement number can occur more than once in an IF statement. In the above example, $N-10$ will never have a value greater than zero as the program will go to statement 3 when it has a zero value.

Some IF statements can be alternatively expressed by means of a computed GO TO statement. The form is:

GO TO (S1, S2, S3, S4, S5, ..., S), i

where S1, S2, etc. are statement numbers and i is an integer variable not greater than the number of statement numbers in the parentheses.

In the sequence of statements:

J = 3
GO TO (6, 15, 8, 6, 9), J

control would be transferred to statement number 8.

Exercises 5.1†

1. Print the integers 1–100 with their square, cube, square root and cube root.
2. Compute and print the reciprocals of the numbers 2–100 to six decimal places.
3. Read 12 sales amounts for 12 months (one amount per card), and print each as a ratio to January with January = 100.
4. Read in ten pairs of numbers representing the smaller sides of ten right-angled triangles, and print the ten values of the hypotenuse. Each pair is punched on a single card.
5. Print a table of circles with areas increasing in steps of a square metre from 1 to 100 square metres and their corresponding radii (assume $\pi = 3.14$).
6. $\pi/4 = 1 - \frac{1}{3} + \frac{1}{5} - \frac{1}{7} + \frac{1}{9}$ ....
   Evaluate 1000 terms of this series and print out the value of π to eight decimal places every 100 terms.
7. Compute and print the terms of the Fibonacci series ($x_{n+1} = x_n + x_{n-1}$) between 10^5 and 10^8. The first few terms are 0 1 1 2 3 5 8 ....
8. The solution of the simultaneous equations

   $ax + by + c = 0$
   $px + qy + r = 0$

   is given by

   $x = (br - cq)/(aq - bp)$
   $y = (pc - ar)/(aq - bp)$

   Read a, b, c, p, q, r and compute and print x and y.
   Print INDETERMINATE if $aq - bp = 0$.
   Print NOT INDEPENDENT if $a/p = b/q = c/r$.

† Suggested solutions to all exercises follow after chapter 8.

Subscripted variables

It is often necessary to perform operations upon tables, sets and similar groups of variables where each member of the group is referred to by the name of the whole group and a suffix or subscript denoting its position within the group, for example,

a_1, x_{ij}

A group of subscripted variables is often called an *array* and the number of items in it must be declared in Fortran by a DIMENSION statement *before* any member of the array is used.

A DIMENSION statement is of the form

DIMENSION a, a, a, ..., a

where each a stands for an array name followed by parentheses enclosing (in the case of the common single-dimensional array) an unsigned integer giving the maximum size of the subscript.

A typical DIMENSION statement could be:

DIMENSION Y(10), B(100), L(25)

This would instruct the compiler to reserve space for 10 Ys, 100 Bs and 25 Ls. Real and integer arrays can be declared in the same DIMENSION statement and there is no limit to the number of these statements in a program. A name used for an array must not be used for any other purpose in the program. As with single variables, the initial letter determines whether the array is real or integer. After the DIMENSION statement, any member of the array can be used in the program. The name of the array is followed by an integer expression denoting the subscript in parentheses. Examples of subscripted variables in arithmetic statements are:

$Y(4) = U - B(18)$
$L(K) = M/I(N)$

A subscript, if i is an integer variable and n an integer constant, can be i, n, $i \pm n$, $n * i$, $n * i \pm n$. Generally simple forms of subscripts should be used by beginners. Some examples in accordance with the above rules could be:

$A(J+3)$
$B(5 * K)$
$E(4 * M - 2)$

A Fortran array can have up to three dimensions. An array with two dimensions is mathematically known as a *matrix* and the element a_{ij} in Fortran would be A(I, J). In data processing, two-dimensional arrays are useful for representing items in rows and columns; the first subscript refers to the row and the second to the column, so that D(2, 3) would refer to the third item in the second row of the table D. DIMENSION statements can include arrays of different dimensions, for example,

DIMENSION V(3, 4), I(85), H(5, 10)

Array V here has three rows and four columns and H has five rows and ten columns.

Triple subscripts are sometimes useful even though they are more difficult to visualize. A simple example would be a table of costs tabulated by product, department and type of cost. This could be declared in Fortran as

DIMENSION ICOST(4, 5, 2)

which would allow for 4 products, 5 departments and 2 types of cost and would have 40 storage locations allocated by the compiler. ICOST(2, 3, 1) would refer to the first type of cost in the third department for the second product. If a card was punched with product, department, type of cost and actual cost value, the value could be added to the appropriate place in the table by the following sequence of statements:

```
    READ 9, I, J, K, ITEM
  9 FORMAT(4(I10))
    ICOST(I, J, K) = ICOST(I, J, K)+ITEM
```

A whole array can be read or printed by one READ or PRINT statement, and with a one-dimensional array this is a satisfactory way of performing the operation. The statements:

```
    DIMENSION X(30)
    READ 2, X
  2 FORMAT(F8.3)
```

would read the 30 elements of the array from the first 8 columns of 30 cards.

If it was desired to punch more than one element per card, a possible sequence of statements would be:

```
    DIMENSION X(30)
    READ 4, X
  4 FORMAT(3(F8.3, 5X))
```

This would read three elements per card.

An array with more than one dimension presents greater difficulties as it is transmitted in the order of the subscript that varies most rapidly. A two-dimensional array, conventionally represented as

A(1, 1) A(1, 2) A(1, 3)
A(2, 1) A(2, 2) A(2, 3)

for 2 rows and 3 columns would be read or printed in the order

A(1, 1) A(2, 1)
A(1, 2) A(2, 2)
A(1, 3) A(2, 3)

If it is desired to read or print an array with more than one dimension in row order, a suitable technique is shown in the section on the implied DO statement.

DO loops

A DO loop provides a more economic method of counting iterations of a sequence of instructions than does the use of a count and the IF statement, which has been the only method of doing this introduced so far. The following program prints the squares and cubes of numbers 1–100 both by a DO loop and by using the IF statement:

(a) Using IF,

```
      N = 1
   2  M = N * N
      L = N * M
      PRINT 1, N, M, L
   1  FORMAT(3(I9, 6X))
      N = N + 1
      IF(N − 101) 2, 3, 3
   3  STOP
      END
```

(b) Using DO loop,

```
      DO 2 N = 1,000
         M = N * N
         L = M * N
      PRINT 1, N, M, L
   1  FORMAT(3(I9, 6X))
   2  CONTINUE
      STOP
      END
```

The DO loop repeats the statements from the statement after the DO up to and including the statement labelled 2 for N taking the values 1–100 increasing in steps of 1. CONTINUE is a statement for which no object program statements are compiled, and in the above example it marks the end of the statements to be executed in the DO loop. The exact use of this statement is explained later.

The general form of the DO loop is

DO h K = M1, M2, M3

where h is the statement number of the last statement in the loop to be executed, K is an integer variable which must not be subscripted, M1 the initial value of the index, M2 the final value and M3 the increment by which the index is increased each time through the loop. If M3 is equal to one (as in the previous example), it may be omitted. K is sometimes known as the controlled variable. M1, M2, M3 are unsigned integer constants or non-subscripted integer variables.

Typical DO loops would be:

DO 18 L = 1, K, 4
DO 9 I = L, M, N
DO 96 J = L, 7, M
DO 5 K = I, K

When the value of the controlled variable exceeds the final value, the loop is said to be satisfied, and control passes to the statement following the end of the DO loop. In the example:

DO 9 I = 2, 9, 5

I would take the values 2 and 7.

The value of the controlled variable is 'undefined' after the DO is satisfied, so no assumption should be made about its value in this circumstance.

The range of the DO can be any number of statements or just a single statement. The DO loop must not begin or end with a statement that is non-executable such as DIMENSION or FORMAT. If we wish to have a statement of this type at the beginning or end, the 'dummy' statement CONTINUE may be used as in the example (b) previously.

The last statement in a DO loop must not be one that changes control (such as IF or GO TO), or another DO.

A GO TO can lead from a DO loop to a statement outside it, but it is forbidden to jump to a statement number in the middle of a DO loop (thus bypassing the indexing parameters at the start) unless it is a return from a temporary exit from the loop. The values of the variables used at the start of the DO loop must not be changed during the execution of the loop.

DO loops can occur within DO loops, and this situation is called a nest of DOs. The only restriction is that the inner DO must be completely within the range of the outer DO. Both can end at the same statement. A statement (such as IF or GO TO) can transfer control from an inner DO to an outer DO, as an inner DO is regarded as being in the range of the outer DO. The following example uses the formula

$$K = ij$$

for ranges of i from 100 to 500 and j from 1 to 10. i is to be increased in steps of 10 and j in steps of 1. A section of program to accomplish this using a nested DO loop is as follows:

```
    DO 9 I = 100, 500, 10
    DO 9 J = 1, 10
       K = (I * J)
  8 FORMAT(I3, 5X, I2, 10X, I8)
  9 PRINT 8, I, J, K
```

Implied DO statement

This is a useful facility for the input and output of arrays in the usual order rather than in the "natural" order mentioned previously in the section on subscripted variables. An implied DO can only appear in an input/output list, and any number of them can appear in a single list. The implied DO is in parentheses; there may be one, two or three sets of parentheses depending on the number of undefined variable subscripts. A simple example of an implied DO would be:

```
    READ 5, (A(J), J = 1, 10)
  5 FORMAT(10(F4.1, 2X))
```

This would read in a whole one-dimensional array from one card.

The technique is more suitable for two- and three-dimensional arrays, which cannot be read in row order by the method discussed previously. A typical use of an implied DO for a two-dimensional array would be:

```
     READ 17, ((X(I, J), J = 1, 2), I = 1, 5)
  17 FORMAT(10(F3.0, 2X))
```

This deals with an array of five rows and two columns, which would be transmitted row by row in the order:

X(1, 1), X(1, 2), X(2, 1), X(2, 2), X(3, 1), X(3, 2), X(4, 1), (X(4, 2), X(5, 1), X(5, 2)

An implied DO for a three-dimensional array could be:
```
     PRINT 5, (((ITEMS(I, J, K), J = 1, 3), K = 1, 2), I = 1, 2)
  5 FORMAT(6(I6, 4X))
```

This would print six numbers to a line in the order

    ITEM(1, 1, 1), ITEM(1, 2, 1), ITEM(1, 3, 1), ITEM(1, 1, 2),
    ITEM(1, 2, 2), ITEM(1, 3, 2)

Any number of subscripted variables can be dealt with in the same implied DO. The statements

    PRINT 6, ((K(I, J), L(I, J), J = 1, 3), I = 1, 2)
6   FORMAT(6(I6, 4X))

would print in the order

    K(1, 1), L(1, 1), K(1, 2), L(1, 2), K(1, 3), L(1, 3),
    K(2, 1), L(2, 1), K(2, 2), L(2, 2), K(2, 3), L(2, 3)

An implied DO can appear in a list with other list items and must be separated from them by commas.

Exercises 5.2

Do questions 1–6 of Exercises 5.1 using DO loops.

Subroutines

It is often necessary to use common sequences of instructions at different points in the program. This idea was demonstrated in chapter 2 where the subroutine concept was defined and illustrated. In Fortran, a subroutine can be regarded as a separate program that is called upon by a statement in the main program or in another subroutine. Subroutines can be compiled independently, which means that once compiled, a subroutine can be used in its compiled form in several programs. This facility of being able to compile subroutines independently is useful in the writing and testing of a large program. Such a program can be divided into subroutines, which can be compiled and tested independently. When all are fully operational, they can be combined together by one small main program, which calls upon each subroutine in turn. Correction of a few small errors could require the recompilation of a large program, and this waste of time may be obviated by the division of a program into subroutines.

When it is required to use a subroutine the statement is

    CALL AB

where AB is the name of the subroutine.

Often the subroutine contains the names of arguments or parameters, which are the quantities upon which it is to perform operations and store results. These must be enclosed in parentheses after the name of the subroutine, for example,

    CALL AB(X, Y, K)

An argument can be a constant, a variable, a subscripted variable, a name of an array without subscripts, an arithmetic expression or a character string like an H format. The following example illustrates all possibilities:

CALL JULIA(K, 7, 3.78, E(5), SET, G+H, 4HDATE)

The name of the actual subroutine is prefaced by SUBROUTINE and is followed by its list of arguments (if any). These arguments are replaced by the actual arguments from the calling program when the program is executed. (To Algol programmers, this is equivalent to 'call by name'.)

If an argument is an array name, it must be given a dimension in the subroutine and must possess the same maximum size as the actual argument in the program that calls it.

The following simple program will illustrate the use of subroutines.

It is desired to read in quantities of millimetres, print these out as metres, centimetres and millimetres and print their average in the same way.

```
      ITOT = 0
      DO 1 I = 1, 10
      READ 2, IMM
  2   FORMAT (I4)
      CALL METRE(IMM, IM, ICM, IM2)
      PRINT 3, IM, ICM, IM2
  3   FORMAT(3(I4, 2X))
  1   ITOT = ITOT + IMM
      IAVE = ITOT/10
      CALL METRE(IAVE, IM, ICM, IM2)
      PRINT 4, IM, ICM, IM2
  4   FORMAT(10HAVERAGE = 3(I2, 2X))
      STOP
      END

      SUBROUTINE METRE(J, K, L, M)

      K = J/1000
      L = J - (1000 * K)
      IF(L) 1, 2, 1
  1   L = L/10
  2   M = J - (1000 * K + 10 * M)
      RETURN
      END
```

It will be seen that the RETURN statement is used whenever it is wished to return to the calling program from the subroutine.

6

There can be any number of RETURN statements in a subroutine.

In the above example, in the first call of METRE, IMM is substituted for J, IM for K, ICM for L and IM2 for M. In the second call IAVE is substituted for J, IM for K, ICM for L and IM2 for M.

Names and labels are local to a subroutine and may be used for a completely different purpose in another subroutine or the main program. The contents of a variable name are not transferred to the same variable name in another subroutine (see *The Common and Equivalence statements* later in this chapter for a further discussion of this). It will be noticed that, in the above example, labels 1 and 2 are used in both the main program and in the subroutine METRE.

The fact that names and labels are local to a particular subroutine facilitates the writing of a large program in the form of several subroutines written by different programmers, since it does not matter if several use the same name or label. Results can be transferred from one subroutine to the main program by means of the parameters. This transfer of value is also discussed later in connection with the COMMON statement.

A program that contains a subroutine (or FUNCTION mentioned in the next section) is said to be *segmented*. Each of the parts of the program is referred to as a *segment*.

Functions

The functions usually supplied in the Fortran compiler such as SQRTF have been mentioned previously in this chapter. If the programmer wishes to write such a function of his own and it can be expressed in a single arithmetic statement, then the facility known as the *arithmetic statement function* may be used.

This must be written before the first executable statement in a program and the name must end in F. It is not usual to begin the name of an arithmetic statement function with X unless the value of the function is an integer.

An example of an arithmetic statement function at the beginning of a program would be

$$SUMSQF(X, Y) = (X+Y) ** 2$$

The function is *not* executed at this point, but only when referred to in the program.

In the above example X and Y are dummy arguments like those encountered in connection with subroutines in the previous section.

A typical reference to the function in the program would be:

$$D = G * H + SUMSQF(R, T)$$

This use of the function in an arithmetic statement would compute the value of the square of $(R+T)$.

The dummy arguments must not contain subscripted variables, and the arithmetic expression on the right-hand side of the function name must not contain subscripted variables.

A function may be used any number of times and may contain a reference to an arithmetic statement function that has been defined above it.

Although a dummy argument is always a simple variable, an actual argument may be a constant, a simple variable, a subscripted variable or an arithmetic expression, for example,

$$E = SUMSQF(R(L), D - 5.9)$$

The arithmetic expression on the right-hand side of an arithmetic function statement may contain variables that are not named as dummy arguments. When the function is used the current value of the variable will be used.

If a function is defined as

$$PRODF(A, B) = A * B * (R + T)$$

in the sequence of instructions

```
R = 7
T = 10
W = PRODF(X, Y)
```

the function will use T with the value 10 and R with the value 7.

Arithmetic statement functions have two serious limitations. They can consist of only one statement and cannot be compiled separately. These limitations can be overcome by using the FUNCTION subprogram, which can be compiled independently of the main program and can consist of several statements.

The form of a FUNCTION is in some ways analogous to that of a SUBROUTINE. It is defined by heading the statements comprising it with the word FUNCTION followed by its name. END is written after the last statement, and whenever it is desired to return to the main program the word RETURN is used.

The FUNCTION name must start with the letters I–N if it is an integer function, A–N or O–Z if it is a real function. If a dummy argument of a function is an array name it must appear in a DIMENSION statement in the function.

A typical function could be:

```
FUNCTION AMEAN(A, N)
DIMENSION A(100)
TOTAL = 0.
DO 1 J = 1, N
```

```
1  TOTAL = TOTAL + A(J)
   B = FLOATF(N)
   AMEAN = TOTAL/B
   RETURN
   END
```

A function can have any number of dummy arguments, which must be non-subscripted variables or array names. The single-value result that is returned to the main program is placed in the name of the function as shown in the above example.

A function is referenced in the program by using its name as an operand in an arithmetic expression, for example,

$$E = 9. + AMEAN(U, J)$$

It was assumed in the FUNCTION AMEAN that the number of elements in the array A would never exceed 100 for an actual argument.

The COMMON and EQUIVALENCE statements

These two non-executable statements are useful in the naming of variables and their assignment to store locations.

It has been explained that each subprogram has its own variable names so that A in the main program is different from A in a SUBROUTINE or FUNCTION. If we wish to use the same variables in two or more segments of a complete program, we can do this by means of a COMMON statement. If we wished to use the variables X, Y and J in three separate program segments, we would have to write the statement

COMMON(X, Y, J)

three times, once for each segment.

The items are variables or non-subscripted array names, and they are given storage in the order in which they appear in the COMMON statement. There may be any number of COMMON statements in a segment. Each starts assignment of storage from where the previous one left off, so in a segment which included the statements

COMMON(U, J, D)
COMMON(P, C, S)

the 'map' of the common storage area would be U, J, D, P, C, S. A subprogram could define these variables in one statement as

COMMON(U, J, D, P, C, S)

If we wish, we can give the same variable storage location different names in different segments by using the COMMON statement. If in two segments the following statements occur:

COMMON(A, B, C)
COMMON(U, V, W)

A and U, B and V, and C and W share the same locations in storage.
The COMMON statement can transmit arguments to and from SUBROUTINES without having explicitly named arguments after the subroutine name. In the following parts of programs:

COMMON(A, B, I, U)
CALL POWER

SUBROUTINE POWER
COMMON(A, B, I, U)
U = (A + B) * I
RETURN
END

the subroutine POWER works on common variables and has no dummy arguments. A FUNCTION, however, must have at least one explicit argument, although it can also utilize the COMMON facility.

If an array name appears in COMMON storage it must also appear in a DIMENSION statement in the same segment, for example with

DIMENSION J(8)
COMMON(I, X, J)

the COMMON storage area would consist of:

I, X, J(1), J(2), J(3), J(4), J(5), J(6), J(7), J(8).

The COMMON statement is very useful when a large program is divided into several subprograms written by different programmers. Variable values requiring transmission between the various subprograms can be placed in previously agreed COMMON variable names.

The EQUIVALENCE statement is another non-executable statement that causes two or more variable names to be assigned to the same storage location, for example,

EQUIVALENCE(A, U, D), (J, N)

will use the same storage locations for A, U, D and J, N. In the following statements:

EQUIVALENCE(A, U, D), (J, N)
D = 3.7
N = 28
N = N + 5

A and U would also have the value 3.7 and J the initial value of 28. Any operation affecting any variable in an EQUIVALENCE statement would affect the other variables in the same parentheses so that J would have the value of 33. This is useful if, in a long program, two similar variable names such as X, X1 have been confused, because we can correct the error by

EQUIVALENCE(X, X1)

and so save having to go back through the program and make many alterations. It is also useful to effect economies in the use of storage when two variables are never needed at the same time.

Variables brought into the COMMON storage area by an EQUIVALENCE statement may reorder the COMMON storage area because the order of the variables in an EQUIVALENCE statement takes precedence, for example in

COMMON(P, Q, R, S)
EQUIVALENCE(R, U), (Q, Z)

the COMMON storage area would be

R, U
Q, Z
P
S

Some versions of Basic Fortran allow references to array items and enable real and integer variables to share the same storage. The reader is referred to the appropriate programming manual for further details of this.

Further FORMAT statements

E format

The E format is useful for reading and printing numbers in a floating-point form, but it is not likely to be greatly used by beginners. The form is

Em.n

where m is the total width of the field and n the number of places assumed to be on the right of the decimal point.

The data are always punched in the form

123456E-2

If this number was read from a card with a FORMAT statement, E9.3, the number would be stored as $123.456 \cdot 10-2 = 1.23456$.

A decimal point can be punched, but if so it overrides the number of places to the right of the point mentioned in the FORMAT statement so that data of the form

345.67E2

read in with the FORMAT statement

E8.4

would be stored as

34567

If a decimal point is punched, then it must be allowed for in the field width. The width must also include E and a sign if the exponent is negative. The maximum number of digits in the exponent is usually two. If minus signs are not punched, the exponent and argument are taken to be positive. No spaces should occur between digits or between digits and the letter E.

If the E format is used for output, the first digit after E stands for the total field width and the second digit for the number of decimal places required in the argument, which is usually (though not on all computers) a decimal fraction greater than or equal in absolute value to 0.1 but less than 1.0. In the following sequence of statements:

$$T = 19.576542$$
$$U = -.0189763$$
PRINT 1, T, U
1   FORMAT(2(E12.5, 4X))

the numbers would be printed as
.19577E 2   .18976E−1

It must be remembered that space must be allowed for a sign for both argument and exponent and also for E and the decimal point, whilst the exponent must have two digit positions. Some versions of Fortran print a zero before the decimal point of the argument; if so a digit position must be allowed for this.

A format

The A format is used for the input and output of alphanumeric characters (a list of such characters in Fortran is commonly called a Hollerith string). The number of these characters that may be read into an integer or real variable varies from one computer to another, and the appropriate programming manual should be consulted. In the IBM 1620, up to four characters may be stored in a real variable, so a typical statement to read the letters CATS into the variable A would be:

    READ 9, A
    9 FORMAT(A4)

The number after A refers to the number of characters to be read from the card.

P format

The P format is used to attach a scale factor to an E or F format specification. These specifications may be preceded by

    nP

where n is an integer specifying the power of ten by which the number is to be multiplied, for example,

    3PE15.5   2PF 7.3

For an F specification, the value is multiplied by the power of ten so that the number 123.456 would be output according to the specification

    2PF8.1

as

    12345.6.

For the E specification, the scale factor moves the decimal point and corrects the exponent so that the number 123.456 would be output according to the specification

    2PR13.5

as

    12.34560E1

Scale factors can be negative for an F specification but are allowed only to be positive in most versions of the language for an E specification. Once a scale factor appears in a FORMAT statement it affects all succeeding E and F specifications in the same FORMAT statement unless another scale factor occurs.

Exercises 5.3

1. Read ten numbers, compute and print the average, and print the number with the greatest absolute deviation from the average.
2. Write a sequence of instructions to divide each element of a matrix with five rows and three columns by the largest element.
3. Write a section of program to print out the largest element of a matrix with three rows and four columns, and also to print out the row and column of the largest element.

4. Print the prime numbers between 3 and 100.
5. Print a square with 19 rows and 19 columns with each of the rows and columns containing once only each of the numbers 1–19 (Latin square).

Some features of A.S.A. Fortran (Fortran IV)

The previous sections have dealt with the features common to the majority of versions of Basic Fortran. Features that have wide variation, such as the magnetic-type instructions, and those that are not common to many compilers, such as IF ACCUMULATOR OVERFLOW and READ DRUM statements, have not been dealt with.

Fortran IV, which was codified in 1966 as A.S.A. Fortran, contains many advanced features not available in Basic Fortran. Some small computers cannot accommodate a compiler for A.S.A. Fortran: the version of Fortran mentioned in the preceding sections of this chapter can therefore be used on both large and small computers.

Below are described some extensions to Basic Fortran found in A.S.A. Fortran.

Type declarations

In A.S.A. Fortran, types may be declared. There are five types of variable: real, integer, double-precision, complex and logical. A variable can be given a type declaration at any point before its use in a program.

REAL ITEM, MEAN
INTEGER   TAX, PAY
DOUBLE PRECISION   TOTAL, SUM (holds a number to twice the precision of a normal variable)

COMPLEX   ROOT, VALUE
LOGICAL   BLONDE, PRETTY (holds a 'truth' value, true or false)

Variable names not defined in a type declaration have their type determined by their initial letter as in Basic Fortran: I–N for integer and A–H and O–Z for real types.

Complex constants are written as a pair of constants separated by a comma and enclosed in brackets, e.g.

(5.9, 20.5) is equal to $5.9 + 20.5i$

Logical constants are .TRUE. and .FALSE.

DATA statement

Data may be compiled into an object program by the DATA statement, which has a list of variables and their values. An example of the DATA statement is

DATA SUM,TOTAL/1.8, 5.4

This would give SUM the value of 1.8 and TOTAL the value of 5.4.

The logical IF statement

In A.S.A. Fortran it is possible to write statements of the type

IF(A.GT.B) GO TO 9

If A is greater than B the program jumps to statement 9, otherwise it obeys the statement following the IF statement.
The relational operators are

.GT.   greater than
.GE.   greater than or equal
.LT.   less than
.LE.   less than or equal
.EQ.   equal
.NE.   not equal

The above relational operators can be combined by the logical operators

.NOT.
.AND.
.OR.
IF(A.LT.B .AND.I.EQ.J) GO TO 5

Parentheses can be used in logical expressions like the above example to indicate the order in which the expression is to be evaluated. If there are no parentheses, the order of the logical operators is .NOT. .AND. .OR.

A LOGICAL variable can be substituted for arithmetic expressions connected by relational operators. The above expression could be alternatively evaluated by the following statements:

LOGICAL E
E = A.LT.B .AND.I.EQ.J
IF(E) GO TO 5

Although it is common to have a GO TO statement to be obeyed if the condition after the IF is true, any single statement except a DO or logical IF statement may be executed.
In the following example:

IF(J.EQ.I) K = K + 1
N = M

K = K + 1 will be executed if the condition is true and then N = M will be obeyed. Similarly, in the sequence of statements:

IF(P.GT.A) CALL AGAIN(P, J)
S = S + H

the subroutine will be obeyed only if the condition is true, and will return to the statement S = S + H.

Dimension statement

A DIMENSION statement in a subprogram may have variable dimensions if the array name and its dimensions are arguments of the subprogram. The actual dimensions appear in the calling program, and these are passed to the subprogram. In this way a subroutine can use arrays whose size is not known until the subroutine is called, for example,

DIMENSION A(30)
CALL OVER (A, 30)

SUBROUTINE OVER(P, J)
DIMENSION P(J)

6

COBOL

The Cobol 1965 Report states that

"Cobol is an industry language and is not the property of any company or group of companies, or of any organization or group of organizations.

No warranty, expressed or implied, is made by any contributor (to the report) or by the Cobol Committee as to the accuracy and functioning of the programming system and language. Moreover, no responsibility is assumed by any contributor, or by the committee, in connection therewith.

Procedures have been established for the maintenance of Cobol. Enquiries concerning the procedures for proposing changes should be directed to the Executive Committee of the Conference on Data Systems Languages.

The authors and copyright holders of the copyrighted material used herein

Flow-matic (trademark for Sperry Rand Corporation), Programming for the Univac (R) I and II, Data Automation Systems copyrighted 1958, 1959, by Sperry Rand Corporation; IBM Commercial Translator Form No. F 28–8013, copyrighted 1959 by IBM; FACT, DSI 27A5260–2760, copyrighted 1960 by Minneapolis–Honeywell

have specifically authorized the use of this material in whole or in part, in the Cobol specifications. Such authorization extends to the reproduction and use of Cobol specifications in programming manuals or similar publications."†

Most present-day computers have Cobol compilers, although there is a certain amount of latitude about which of the 'elective' features allowed in the Cobol-61 report are implemented. The interested user is advised to consult the appropriate Cobol manual to ascertain which elective features are allowed.

In 1963, the European Computer Manufacturer's Association (E.C.M.A.) produced proposals for "Compact Cobol", which consists of the essential features of Cobol and which can be implemented on small computers. The version of Cobol given in this chapter is based on Compact Cobol, which is a sub-set of full Cobol and is compatible with it.

† The Cobol 1965 Report, issued by the U.S. Department of Defense.

Basic elements

The character set of Cobol is as follows:

numerals 0–9	/	;
letters A–Z	=	"
space	£	( )
+	$	>
−	.	<
*	,	

Non-numeric literals can contain other characters besides these (see later). Cobol words can be classified into two types: *key* words and *optional* words. In this text, key words are italicized to remind the reader that they must be copied exactly (without of course the italics) and cannot be omitted. Key words are sometimes referred to as *reserved* words. Cobol names can be combined to form sentences, and sentences can be combined to form paragraphs. Cobol is usually punched on cards in the following format:

Columns 1–3 contain a page number.
Columns 4–6 contain a line number.
Paragraph headings commence in column 8.   (Margin A)
Sentences commence in column 12.   (Margin B)
Column 7 is blank except when a card is a continuation of the previous one.
Columns 73–80 are used for any comment or identification meaningful to the programmer.

A Cobol program has four divisions. The *identification* division gives the program a title; the *environment* division describes the computers on which the program is to be compiled and executed; the *data* division describes the structure of the data used in the program, and the *procedure* division contains the instructions of the program.

Identification division

The structure of the identification is:

IDENTIFICATION DIVISION.
PROGRAM-ID. Program-name.
Other information, e.g. date.

The program name must begin with a letter, and the rest must be alphabetic or numeric. The number of characters permitted in a program-name varies from one compiler to another.
The full stops and hyphen must *not* be omitted.

Environment division

The structure of the environment division is:

ENVIRONMENT DIVISION.
CONFIGURATION SECTION.
SOURCE-COMPUTER.   Source computer-name.
OBJECT-COMPUTER.   Object computer-name.
INPUT-OUTPUT SECTION.
FILE-CONTROL.

The source-computer entry names the computer on which the program is to be compiled; in the majority of cases this is the same computer as that on which the object program is to be executed. It is useful, however, to be able to compile a program for a small computer that could not itself hold the compiler. It is sometimes necessary to give a more detailed description of the source- and object-computers. The appropriate Cobol programming manual will supply further information if this is needed.

After the heading *FILE-CONTROL*, entries of the following format are used:

SELECT file-name *ASSIGN* hardware-name.

The file-name is a data-name and is used also in the data division where the structure of the file will be described.

The hardware-names to describe the paper-tape reader, card reader and magnetic file devices for a particular computer vary with each compiler. A typical entry in the file-control section would be:

ENVIRONMENT DIVISION.
CONFIGURATION SECTION.
SOURCE-COMPUTER.   ABC 1899.
OBJECT-COMPUTER.   XYZ 1984.
INPUT-OUTPUT SECTION.
FILE-CONTROL.
     SELECT STOCKIN *ASSIGN* CARD-READER 1.
     SELECT PRODUCT1 *ASSIGN* TAPE 1.
     SELECT PRODUCT2 *ASSIGN* TAPE 2.
     SELECT TABLE *ASSIGN* PRINTER 1.

Data division

Each item of data to be processed by the program instructions in the procedure division must be named and defined in the data division. The three major sections of this division deal with files, working-storage and constants. Some compilers also have LINKAGE and REPORT sections, which are elective features. The fact that the data division is separate from the program instructions in the procedure division makes possible the alteration of one division without the other. In a large commercial application needing many programs that use some common files, parts of the data division of one program may be used in another.

The rules for forming Cobol names and constants will now be presented as both will be needed in the data division. Names have already been encountered in the case of the program-name and file-names. Generally, data-names must begin with an alphabetic character. The usual character set for names is:

0–9
A–Z
hyphen (-)

Examples would be

TAX, WAGE, ACCOUNT-31, NET-TOTAL, COUNTS.

Names must not end with a hyphen or contain a space, since a space is used to terminate a name. The number of characters allowed to form a name varies from one compiler to another. (Procedure-names are mentioned in the next section.)

Reserved words must not be used for data-names. Avoidance of reserved words can be difficult, but since none contain a digit, if every data-name contains a digit a programmer can be sure of not inadvertently using a reserved word.

Constants consist of numeric literals, non-numeric literals and figurative constants. A numeric literal may contain only the numerals 0–9, +, − and the decimal point. It can contain one sign, one decimal point, or a sign and a decimal point. If there is no sign the literal is assumed to be positive.

The decimal point may be punched anywhere except at the extreme right of a number, so that 1234. would not (unlike Fortran) be a valid literal. Insignificant zeros are ignored. The number of digits allowed varies according to the computer used. If a sign is present, there must *not* be a blank card column between the sign and the first digit. Examples of valid literals are:

14 +9 −10 0005 .76 0.89 +00.0029

Non-numeric literals contain any character except the prime and are always enclosed in primes. They must *not* be used for computation and are usually used when phrases are to be printed. A blank can be included as part of the literal. The maximum length of a non-numeric literal is usually 120 characters. Typical non-numeric literals would be:

"STOCK BALANCE" "6 OCTOBER 1967"

Figurative constants consist of fixed data-names that have been given to frequently used constants. Useful ones are

ZERO   ZEROS   ZEROES
SPACE   SPACES

These will give a series of one or more zeros or spaces depending on the context.

The file section of the data division assumes that all data defined therein are grouped in *files*. Thus in the simple commercial application of updating a stock file from movement cards and printing out details of stocks that have fallen below re-order level, file definitions would be needed for the input cards and the lines printed as well as for the magnetic-tape stock files.

Files are considered as being subdivided into *records* which in turn are subdivided into items. For the input-card file mentioned above, the record name could be STOCKCARD and the item-names on the card could be STOCKNO QUANT. Items are often split into subitems which can in turn be further divided. Items which are further subdivided are called *elementary items*.

In order to define groups of items, level numbers are used. Level one is the record, and the numbers 02–49 refer to items in their hierarchical order. An item of data contains within it all items directly below it that have larger level numbers. Division into levels allows a programmer to deal at will with a whole record, group of items or elementary items. In some compilers, levels 77 and 88 are used for special purposes, and the appropriate programming manual must be consulted for details of this facility.

An example of division into levels could be

```
01  NAMECARD
    02  NAME
        03  SURNAME
        03  INITIALS
    02  ADDRESS
        03  NUMBER
        03  ROAD
        03  AREA
            04  TOWN
            04  COUNTY
            04  COUNTRY.
```

A programmer has a great deal of freedom as to how he subdivides records and is not fettered by physical characteristics such as the relationship of a record to the amount of data held on a punched card or block of magnetic tape.

File description

The first section of the data division deals with file structure and is known as the file description. A file description is a sentence with the following format:

> *FD* file-name
> *RECORDING MODE IS* mode
> *BLOCK* integer *RECORDS* or *CHARACTERS*
> *LABEL RECORDS STANDARD* or *OMITTED*
> *VALUE OF* data-name *IS* literal-1
> *DATA RECORDS* data-name

These clauses will now be examined in greater detail. A typical file description would be:

> *FD* STOCK1
> *BLOCK* 4 *RECORDS*
> *LABEL RECORDS STANDARD*
> *DATA RECORDS* STOCKA, STOCKB.

It will be noticed that some of the clauses mentioned in the format description of the file description can be omitted.

1. *FD* file-name
   This gives a name to the file which must have previously appeared in the input-output section of the environment division after *SELECT*. Each file description in the data division commences with *FD*.

2. *RECORDING MODE*
   In many computers there is only one mode of recording information and in this case the *RECORDING MODE* clause need not be used. When more than one mode is possible, the appropriate Cobol programming manual will give full information.

3. *BLOCK* n *CHARACTERS* (or n *RECORDS*)
   This gives the compiler the size of the input or output area associated with an individual file. In the case of a punched card file or a printer file, the *CHARACTERS* option is used to indicate the maximum number of card columns or print positions starting from position (or column) 1. In the majority of cases when a paper-tape file is used the *CHARACTERS* option will be used, but when paper tape is used in a manner analogous to magnetic tape then the *RECORDS* option will be preferred. Magnetic files use the *RECORDS* option, and the details of use can be found in the appropriate Cobol manual.

7

4. *LABEL RECORDS STANDARD* (or *OMITTED*)

This clause may be omitted for other than magnetic-tape files. Magnetic-tape files are usually described as possessing *STANDARD* labels, so that the usual method of tape labelling and checking used by the operating system of a particular computer can be utilized: otherwise the programmer must write his own labelling and checking instructions.

5. *VALUE OF*

This gives the value of individual items on a standard file label and has no significance elsewhere. The non-numeric literals following are individual to a particular compiler.

6. *DATA RECORDS*

This lists every type of record in the file. The entries need not be in the same order as the record descriptions but must all have level 01 entries in the record description.

The record description must now be considered. Each file description must be followed by a record description defining the structure of each record mentioned in the *DATA RECORDS* clause.

The general structure of each sentence in the record description is:

Level number   data-name (or *FILLER*)   optional clauses.

This structure will now be reviewed in detail.

Record description

1. *Level number*

This indicates whether a name refers to a record, group of items or an elementary item. The concept of levels has been described previously in this chapter. An item includes all items described below it until a level number greater than or equal to its own level number is encountered.

2. Data-name (or *FILLER*)

If no reference is made to an item in the procedure division the word *FILLER* is used. It must be accompanied by a clause describing the form of the data thus described.

The optional clauses are as follows:

1. *REDEFINES* data-name

This option allows the area of storage allocated to the data-name before *REDEFINES* to be shared by the data-name after. The level numbers of the two data-names must be the same, and except in the working storage and constants section must not be 01. Since the amount of computer storage used by both names must be identical, familiarity with the storage allocation method of a particular compiler is implied.

2. *SIZE* n *CHARACTERS* (or *DIGITS*)

This determines the size of an elementary item: n is an unsigned integer. The size varies with the class and usage of the item, and reference must be made to the appropriate Cobol manual. If *SIZE* and *PICTURE* occur in the same sentence, the *PICTURE* determines the size.

3. USAGE *COMPUTATIONAL* (or *DISPLAY*)

This is used to represent the manner in which the data are to be held. *COMPUTATIONAL* is used for data used in calculations and *DISPLAY* for data used for printing such as a name and address. There are many individual variants, such as *COMPUTATIONAL-1*, which deal with the precision and mode in which numeric information is to be held. The appropriate programming manual should *always* be consulted for details of the USAGE clause.

4. *OCCURS* n *TIMES* (n is an unsigned integer)

This is used to reserve storage space for identical items or subscripted variables, for example,

04 MESSAGE
SIZE 6 *CHARACTERS DISPLAY*
OCCURS 4 *TIMES*.

would reserve for four items of six characters. Items thus described are referred to in the procedure division by subscripts.

It may be helpful to see how subscripts are referred to in the procedure division. Subscripts themselves must be data-names or literals and cannot themselves be subscripted.

CODE (4) in the procedure division would refer to the fourth member of the set defined as CODE with *OCCURS*. CODE (I) would refer to the Ith member of the set. *OCCURS* cannot be used for records (level 1 items).

Some Cobol compilers permit double and triple subscripts. If it was desired to define a table with five rows and three columns the description would be

02 TABLE
03 COLUMN *OCCURS* 3 *TIMES*.
04 ROW *OCCURS* 5 *TIMES SIZE* 4 *DIGITS*.

Individual items in this TABLE would be referred to as ROW (m, n) where m and n are integers or data names and m refers to the column and n to the row. ROW (2, 4) would refer to the second column of the fourth row.

5. *CLASS NUMERIC*
   ALPHABETIC
   ALPHANUMERIC

This clause describes the type of data in a field. (*AN* is an abbreviated form of *ALPHANUMERIC*)
   If this clause is written at the group level (i.e. to describe an item that is further subdivided into elementary items), the description applies to all elementary items in the group. No individual *PICTURE* clause may contradict the information in the *CLASS* clause. In some compilers the class is implicitly derived from the *PICTURE* clause and a separate *CLASS* clause is not then essential. Naturally a *COMPUTATIONAL* item must always be classed as *NUMERIC*, and class need not be defined for an item specified as *COMPUTATIONAL*.

6. *SYNCHRONIZED LEFT* (or *RIGHT*)

This clause is used with a fixed-length word computer to describe data in such a way as to occupy the minimum amount of storage. Detailed advice as to the use of the clause should be found from the appropriate Cobol manual.

7. *JUSTIFIED LEFT* (or *RIGHT*)

This clause can be used when data are being moved to storage space larger than the data themselves. If this clause is not used, integer computational data are normally right-justified with vacant digit positions to the left of the data filled out with zeros; numeric data with decimal parts are positioned according to the assumed decimal point with unused positions to the right or left filled out with zeros, and alphabetic or alphanumeric data are left-justified with spaces occupying unused positions to the right of the data. The *JUSTIFIED* clause usually overrides this positioning, but there are variations with individual compilers.

8. *POINT LEFT* (or *RIGHT*) n *PLACES* (n is an unsigned integer)

This clause must be used only to describe an elementary numeric item; it indicates the assumed position of the decimal point in relation to the least significant digit of the data.

   POINT LEFT 2 *PLACES*

could be used to describe an item using two decimal places such as dollars and cents.

The *RIGHT* option is less used: it indicates that the assumed decimal point lies outside the item so that actual data 789 with the clause

POINT RIGHT 3 *PLACES*

would be treated as if it were 789000. There is little purpose in using the *POINT* clause when the item is described by a *PICTURE* clause.

9. *SIGNED*
   This clause indicates that an elementary numeric item has a + or − associated with it in storage. *NUMERIC* need not be used when *SIGNED* is present. However, *SIGNED* is rarely used, since this information is invariably given in the *PICTURE* clause.

Record description: *the PICTURE clause*
   Reference has been made frequently in the previous section to this clause, which describes the characteristics of an elementary item in such a way as to make superfluous some clauses like *POINT*. The format of the clause is:

   PICTURE   series of characters.

The characters which follow *PICTURE* are discussed in detail below.

   PICTURE clauses are the simplest and most convenient way of describing data and are less clumsy than some of the clauses mentioned previously. For instance, the following clauses:

SIZE 4 *DIGITS*   *CLASS NUMERIC POINT RIGHT* 2 *PLACES*
   SIGNED

may be expressed briefly in a *PICTURE* clause as

PICTURE S99V99

PICTURE clauses are used both to describe the characteristics of an elementary item of data and to specify how data are to be edited before printing.

1. Non-edited numeric items
   Basically, each digit in the data is represented by 9 so that an item of five digits would be described by

   PICTURE 99999

   It is not necessary to write a long string of 9s since the above clause could be expressed more concisely as

   PICTURE 9(5)

This simplification can be used with other characters besides 9 as will be seen later.

If a numeric item may be positive or negative, the first character after *PICTURE* must be S, for example,

PICTURE S999

The position of a decimal point in an item containing a fractional part is indicated by V. An item containing three decimal places could be described by:

PICTURE S99V999

If the decimal point does not lie immediately to the left or right of an item, P can be used in the description.

PICTURE 99PP

could represent a number such as 7500 and

PICTURE VPP9999 (or VP(2)9(4))

could represent a number such as .001234.

2. Non-edited alphabetic and alphanumeric items

An item containing only letters of the alphabet can be designated in a *PICTURE* clause with the character A, for example,

PICTURE AAAAA (or A(5)).

If the item contains both letters and numbers, X can be used to represent any acceptable character in the character set of the particular computer used, for example,

PICTURE XXXXXX (or X(6)).

3. Edited data

It is often desired to insert or replace characters in data before printing. The character Z in a *PICTURE* clause specifies suppression of leading zeros. Leading zeros may be replaced by spaces by replacing leading 9s by Zs. For example,

PICTURE ZZ999

would print 06789 as 6789 and 00020 as 020. If the *PICTURE* clause contains only Zs and the value of the data is zero, then the edited item will be all spaces.

Various symbols can be added to the data in an elementary item by inserting the required symbols in the *PICTURE* clause. + or − can be

written as the first or last character in a description. CR or DB can be
written as the last two characters if the item is negative
    If it is desired to have zero suppression with the sign 'floated' in front of
the most significant digit, the sign is inserted in the *PICTURE* clause in
each leading position to be suppressed. This applies only if more than one
sign is written.
    If − is written in the description, the sign is printed only if the data are
negative. If + is written, + is inserted if the data are positive and − if
they are negative. Examples of the effect of signs, CR and DB are given
below:

Item	*Picture*	*Edited value*
− 123	− 999	− 123
− 123	999 −	123 −
123	− 999	123
− 12	− 999	− 012
− 7	− − 99	− 07
− 7	− − − 9	− 7
0	− − − −	(blank)
− 123	+ 999	− 123
123	+ 999	+ 123
123	999 +	123 +
9	+ + 99	+ 09
0	+ + + +	(blank)
123	999CR	123
− 123	999CR	123CR
123	999DB	123
− 123	999DB	123DB

A £ (or $) symbol can be inserted in the *PICTURE* clause as the left-hand
character. If it is desired to 'float' the symbol, the symbol is repeated in a
manner similar to + and −.

Item	*Picture*	*Edited value*
123	£999	£123
23	£999	£023
3	£ZZ9	£ 3
0	£ZZZ	(blank)
23	££99	£ 23
0	££££	(blank)
0	££99	£ 00

An asterisk (∗) can be used instead of Z for cheque protection by replacing
leading zeros by asterisks. The clause

    PICTURE ∗∗∗∗

would edit data of value 123 as ∗123 and of value 0 as ∗∗∗∗.

Commas, decimal points, spaces and zeros can be inserted in numeric elementary items by using a *PICTURE* sign containing respectively , ,(Vor.), B and 0.

There are variants for the insertion of a decimal point in data, and the reader should consult the appropriate Cobol programming manual for the form in a particular compiler. Examples of the use of some insertion characters are given below.

Item	Picture	Edited value
123	90099	10023
3	ZZZ00	300
123	9B9B9	1 2 3
1234	9,999	1,234
34	Z,Z99	34
34	9,999	0,034
0	Z,ZZZ	(blank)
123	99.9	12.3

File section example

The following example describes files for an ingenuous stock file updating system where it is required to read stock movements from punched cards, make an updated copy of the master file and print reports for items with stock below recorder level.

   DATA DIVISION.
   FILE SECTION.
   FD STOCK-A *BLOCK CONTAINS* 10 *RECORDS LABEL*
      RECORDS STANDARD VALUE OF FILE-ID IS "STOCKM"
      DATA RECORDS STOCK.
  01 STOCK.
     02 CODE *PICTURE* 9(6).
     02 DESC *PICTURE* X(20).
     02 BAL *PICTURE* 9999.
     02 RLEVEL *PICTURE* 9999.

   FD STOCK-B *BLOCK CONTAINS* 10 *RECORDS LABEL*
      RECORDS STANDARD VALUE OF FILE-ID IS "STOCKM"
      DATA RECORDS STOCK1.
  01 STOCK1.
     02 CODE1 *PICTURE* 9(6).
     02 DESC1 *PICTURE* X(20).
     02 BAL1 *PICTURE* 9999.
     02 RLEVEL1 *PICTURE* 9999.

FD STOCKS *BLOCK CONTAINS* 80 *CHARACTERS LABEL
RECORDS OMITTED DATA RECORDS* STOCKS.

01 STOCKS.
    02 PART *PICTURE* 9(6).
    02 *FILLER PICTURE* XXXX.
    02 MOVT *PICTURE* 999.
    02 *FILLER PICTURE* X(67).

FD REPORT *BLOCK CONTAINS* 120 *CHARACTERS LABEL
RECORDS OMITTED DATA RECORDS* TITLE, SHORT.

01 TITLE.
    02 DATE *PICTURE* Z9BB99BB99.
    02 *FILLER PICTURE* X(30).
    02 HEADER *PICTURE* X(10).
    02 *FILLER PICTURE* X(70).

01 SHORT.
    02 *FILLER PICTURE* X(20).
    02 NUMB *PICTURE* 9(6).
    02 *FILLER PICTURE* X(5).
    02 KIND *PICTURE* X(20).
    02 *FILLER PICTURE* X(5).
    02 AMOUNT *PICTURE* ZZZ9.

Exercises 6.1†

1. A card has employee numbers in columns 1–5, hours in columns 10–11, overtime in columns 20–21. Prepare a record description WEEKLY for this.

2. A record on magnetic tape called AMOUNT contains the following items; prepare a record description.
   (a) SALES six digits with two decimal places.
   (b) MONTH two digits.
   (c) CHANGES three digits signed.
   (d) NAME 20 alphabetic characters.
   (e) KIND eight alphanumeric characters.
   (f) REPCODE three digits.
   (g) AREA four alphanumeric characters.

3. A card contains an alphabetic part in columns 1–8, quantity in columns 9–13, numeric type in columns 14–16, alphanumeric description in columns 17–32 and price in columns 33–36. Write a record description STOCK for this.

† Suggested solutions to all exercises follow after chapter 8.

4. A stock record on magnetic tape consists of a stock number composed of a three-digit type number and a three-digit unit number; a 20-character alphanumeric description; four-digit balance; four-digit re-order level, and a four-digit purchasing code composed of a two-digit area number and a two-digit supplier number. Write a record description for this.

5. A record, PRINT-LINE, contains the following items. Write a record description that will include the appropriate editing.

Source item picture	Name	Print positions	Editing needed
99999	CODE	7–11	Suppress leading zeros
A(20)	NAME	16–37	None
99	AREA1	44–45	Suppress leading zeros
999	AREA2	49–51	Suppress leading zeros
99999	NUMBER	56–60	Suppress leading zeros
99	MONTH	64–65	Suppress leading zeros
99	DAY	68–69	Suppress leading zeros
9999	AMOUNT	74–78	Print £ immediately to the left of left-hand digit

Data division: working storage

In most programs some working space is needed for storage of intermediate results. In the Cobol data division, working storage is described in a similar manner to record storage. In some cases parts of the working store are organized into records with groups of elementary items, but the most common items in working storage are elementary items that form a 'scratch-pad' for intermediate results. All the descriptive clauses used to describe file records can be used in the working section.

The VALUE is especially useful in the working-storage section to specify an initial value for elementary items, for example,

01   TOTAL *PICTURE* 9999 *VALUE ZERO*.
01   PI *PICTURE* 9V99 *VALUE* 3.14.

The working-storage section is always preceded by the title *WORKING-STORAGE SECTION*.
A typical storage section is given below.

WORKING-STORAGE SECTION.
01   TEMPREC.
    02   QUANT *PICTURE* 9999.
    02   PRICE *PICTURE* 999.
01   TOTALA *PICTURE* 999.
01   TOTALB *PICTURE* 99 *VALUE ZERO*
01   HEADER *PICTURE* X(5) *VALUE* "MONTH".

Constant section

A programmer sometimes wishes to give constants a name and to refer to them by this name rather than by the actual value. Items are given descriptive clauses, and the constant is inserted in the item by a *VALUE* clause. A typical constant section could be:

CONSTANT SECTION.
01 TIME
02 MONTH *PICTURE* X(4) *VALUE* "JUNE".
02 YEAR *PICTURE* 9(2) *VALUE* "68".
01 COUNTRY *PICTURE* X(6) *VALUE* "SUSSEX".
01 RATE *PICTURE* V999 *VALUE* .025.

Procedure division: arithmetic verbs

The procedure division contains the actual instructions for computation and manipulation of data. It is analogous to the program statements of Algol and Fortran. It is always headed by the words

PROCEDURE DIVISION.

This division consists of one or more paragraphs. A paragraph starts with the paragraph name and consists then of one or more sentences. A section consists of several paragraphs.

A Cobol sentence usually consists of one or more statements ended by a full stop. Statements can be separated from one another by THEN, a comma or a semi-colon.

A statement is an imperative statement or a conditional statement. In this section some imperative statements will be considered. These statements begin with a verb such as *ADD*.

To clarify the above remarks about the structure of the procedure division, a short opening paragraph is given below.

PROCEDURE DIVISION.
TOTAL.
READ STOCK, *AT END GO TO* BALANCE. *ADD* Q *TO* TOTQ.
ADD PRICE *TO* TOTP. *ADD* 1 *TO* COUNT.

The form of the *ADD* instruction is:

$$ADD \left\{ \begin{array}{c} \text{literal 1} \\ \text{data-name 1} \end{array} \right\} \left[\begin{array}{c} \text{,literal 2...} \\ \text{data-name 2} \end{array} \right] \begin{array}{c} TO \\ GIVING \end{array} \text{data-name n}$$

The following examples will clarify the above structure.

ADD PRICE *TO* TOTAL.
ADD 100 *TO* SUM.
ADD BASIC, BONUS *GIVING* SALARY.
ADD COUNT, 1 *GIVING* NEWCOUNT.
ADD PRICE, DELCHARGE, TAX *GIVING* NETT.

The comma may be replaced by AND, or both the comma and AND may be used, for example,

ADD PRICE AND DELCHARGE AND TAX *GIVING* NETT.
ADD PRICE, DELCHARGE, AND TAX *GIVING* NETT.

Addition is performed algebraically. The contents of the name after *TO* or *GIVING* is altered since the name contains the result of the addition. The contents of the other names used in the instruction remain unaltered.

Two options can follow either form of the *ADD* instruction; indeed they can be used with any of the four arithmetic verbs. These options are *ROUNDED* and ON *SIZE ERROR*.

If the result of an arithmetic operation has more decimal places than were defined in the name receiving the result, the extra decimal places are dropped (truncation). This can be prevented by the use of the *ROUNDED* option. If this is used, the least significant digit of the resultant data-name has its value increased by 1 whenever the most significant digit of the excess which cannot be accommodated is greater than, or equal to, 5.

Whenever an arithmetic result exceeds the number of integral places (those to the left of the decimal point) associated with the resultant data-name, a size-error condition arises. If this occurs when the ON *SIZE ERROR* option is not used, the action taken depends on the particular compiler used; sometimes the most significant digits of the result are lost, and the program continues. If the option is used, the statement after the word *ERROR* will be executed. Any imperative statement may occur here, for example,

ADD ITEM *TO* SUM ON *SIZE ERROR GO TO* OUT.

The form of the subtract instruction is

$$SUBTRACT \left\{ \begin{array}{c} \text{literal 1} \\ \text{data-name} \end{array} \right\} \left[\begin{array}{c} \text{,literal 2...} \\ \text{data-name 2} \end{array} \right] FROM \left\{ \begin{array}{c} \text{literal n} \\ \text{data-name n} \end{array} \right\}$$

[*GIVING* data-name n]   [*ROUNDED*]   [,ON *SIZE ERROR*
                                            imperative statement.]

The *GIVING* option is used when it is desired to subtract one data item from another and store the result in yet another data area so that the two operands of the *SUBTRACT* are unchanged.

The form for multiplication is

$$MULTIPLY \left\{ \begin{array}{c} \text{literal 1} \\ \text{data-name 1} \end{array} \right\} BY \left\{ \begin{array}{c} \text{,literal 2} \\ \text{data-name 2} \end{array} \right\} \begin{array}{c} [GIVING \\ \text{data-name 3}] \end{array}$$

[*ROUNDED*] [,ON *SIZE ERROR* imperative statement].

If the *GIVING* option is not used to identify the product area, the product will replace the multiplier (second data-name), which must not be a literal.

The form for division is as follows

$$DIVIDE \left\{ \begin{array}{l} \text{literal 1} \\ \text{data-name 1} \end{array} \right\} INTO \left\{ \begin{array}{l} \text{literal 2} \\ \text{data-name 2} \end{array} \right\} \begin{array}{l} [GIVING \\ \text{data-name 3}] \end{array}$$

[*ROUNDED*] [,ON *SIZE ERROR* imperative statement].

If the *GIVING* option is not used, the second operand stores the result and must not be a literal.

The following table summarizes the action of some of the alternative forms of the arithmetic verbs.

Statement	*Value after execution*			
	W	X	Y	Z
ADD W *TO* X	W	W + X		
ADD W, X	W	W + X		
ADD W, X, Y, Z	W	X	Y	W + X + Y + Z
ADD W, X, Y *TO* Z	W	X	Y	W + X + Y + Z
ADD W, X, Y *GIVING* Z	W	X	Y	W + X + Y
SUBTRACT X *FROM* Y		X	Y − X	
SUBTRACT X, Y *FROM* Z		X	Y	Z − (X + Y)
SUBTRACT W, X *FROM* Y *GIVING* Z	W	X	Y	Y − (W + X)
MULTIPLY W *BY* X	W	WX		
MULTIPLY W *BY* X *GIVING* Y	W	X	WX	
DIVIDE W *INTO* X	W	X/W		
DIVIDE W *INTO* X *GIVING* Y	W	X	X/W	

In any application requiring complicated arithmetic operations, the use of arithmetic verbs can produce a very verbose program. Sometimes in commercial programs statistical formulae are needed, and the use of these with arithmetic verbs would result in very cumbersome statements. A more elegant alternative method of expressing such formulae utilizes the *COMPUTE* facility. The form is

$$COMPUTE \text{ data-name 1 } [ROUNDED] \left\{ \begin{array}{l} = \\ EQUALS \end{array} \right\} \text{arithmetic}$$

expression [, ON *SIZE ERROR* imperative statement].

In some Cobol manuals, the arithmetic expression is called a formula. Readability and the character set of the particular compiler used determine which of the alternatives are used for =.

An arithmetic expression can be defined as any meaningful combination of data-names, numeric literals and arithmetic operators. The usual forms for arithmetic operators are

+

−

*   (multiplication)
/   (division)
** (exponentiation; raised to the power of; A ** 3 = A cubed)

Parentheses can be used as in algebraic formulae. If parentheses are not used all exponentiations are done first, followed by multiplications and divisions, and finally additions and subtractions.
Thus the expression

$$T + U/V + W * X ** Y - Z$$

would be treated by the Cobol compiler as though written as

$$T + (U/V) + (W * (X ** Y)) - Z.$$

Subject to the above hierarchy, operations are performed in an arithmetic expression from left to right. The programmer is strongly urged to use parentheses when there is any doubt whatsoever about the order in which an arithmetic expression will be evaluated. Some examples of the *COMPUTE* verb are given below:

> *COMPUTE* TIME = HOURS + OVERTIME.
> *COMPUTE* SUM-OF-Y = SUM-OF-Y + Y.
> *COMPUTE* E = X * (C + D).
> *COMPUTE* CHARGE = (1.00 + RATE) ** T.

The *MOVE* verb is used for the transmission of data from one area to another. Editing may take place in the transfer if this is specified in the data-division description of the area to which the data are being moved.

When a numeric elementary item or literal is moved, the item is aligned according to the position of the decimal point in the receiving data area. Zeros are filled in at either end if the item being moved is smaller than the receiving data area unless editing is specified in the data description in that area. Truncation will occur if the receiving area is too small. When a non-numeric item is moved, the receiving area is filled from left to right and unused portions of the area are filled out with spaces.

The form of the instruction is

$$MOVE \left\{ \begin{array}{l} \text{data-name 1} \\ \text{literal} \\ \text{figurative constant} \end{array} \right\} TO \text{ data-name 2 [,data-name 3]}$$
$$\text{[,data-name n].}$$

The options are used when it is desired to move data to more than one receiving area.

The following examples will clarify the action of *MOVE*. The statement

MOVE FIELD *TO* FIELD-1, FIELD-2, FIELD-3, FIELD-4.

with data items described as

01 FIELD   *PICTURE* 99999V999.
01 FIELD-1 *PICTURE* 9V99999.
01 FIELD-2 *PICTURE* 99999.
01 FIELD-3 *PICTURE* 999999V99.
01 FIELD-4 *PICTURE* 999999V99999.

and FIELD containing 23456.789 would give:

FIELD-1 6.78900
FIELD-2 23456
FIELD-3 023456.78
FIELD-4 023456.78900

The statement

MOVE NAME *TO* NAME-1, NAME-2, NAME-3.

with data items described as

01 NAME   *PICTURE* XXXXXX.
01 NAME-1 *PICTURE* XXXX.
01 NAME-2 *PICTURE* XX.
01 NAME-3 *PICTURE* XXXXXXXX.

and NAME containing ABCDEF would give:

NAME-1 ABCD
NAME-2 AB
NAME-3 ABCDEF   (2 spaces on the right).

It is sometimes required to break away from the normal statement-by-statement sequence in which a Cobol program is executed. A *GO TO* verb jumps to the name of a paragraph or section and recommences executing the program statement by statement from that point, for example,

GO TO CALCULATE

would obey the first statement in the paragraph or section named CALCULATE and then obey statements sequentially from that point onwards.

A *GO TO* statement must be the only verb or the last verb in a sentence.

The form of the statement is

GO TO procedure-name.

There are two forms of the *STOP* statement:

$$STOP \begin{cases} literal \\ RUN \end{cases}$$

The former is used when we wish to have a temporary halt in a program for some kind of operator intervention. The literal is displayed in some form on the console so that the operator can identify the particular halt-point and take the appropriate action. The program can be restarted at the next statement. The *STOP RUN* option is used when restart not required.

Conditional statements

One of the most powerful features of a digital computer is the power to transfer control to various parts of the program according to a decision taken by the computer itself. For instance, an instruction can determine if the stock balance has fallen below re-order level and if so can jump to the appropriate part of the program to print out a message that stock should be reordered.

The basic structure of a simple Cobol conditional statement is

IF   condition   statement(s).

An example could be

IF BALANCE IS *LESS* THAN RELEVEL *GO TO* REORDER.

The structure of a condition is

arithmetic expression   relational operator   arithmetic expression

If the condition after the *IF* is untrue, the rest of the sentence will be ignored. (It will be noticed that the IS is not italicized and is merely a "noise-word" to make the program more readable. IS can be used in many parts of a program to enhance comprehensibility.)

The forms of the relational operator are:

[*NOT*] *GREATER* THAN
[*NOT*] *LESS* THAN
[*NOT*] *EQUAL TO*
UNEQUAL TO
EQUALS
EXCEEDS

On either side of the relational operator can be a name, literal or arithmetic expression. The last three relations listed above are alternatives provided for flexibility. Numeric items are compared algebraically. For non-numeric items, reference should be made to the appropriate manufacturer's Cobol manual for the numeric value of the various characters.

Only elementary items and items of the same class (i.e. numeric or non-numeric) can be compared. We sometimes wish to see if a data-name that could contain either letters or digits contains only one or the other. There is a form of the *IF* statement that will test the class of such an item. The form is given below:

$$IF \text{ data-name IS } [NOT] \left\{ \begin{array}{l} NUMERIC \\ ALPHABETIC \end{array} \right\}$$

Another useful form of the *IF* statement is

$$IF \left\{ \begin{array}{l} \text{data-name} \\ \text{arithmetic expression} \end{array} \right\} \text{ IS } [NOT] \left\{ \begin{array}{l} POSITIVE \\ NEGATIVE \\ ZERO \end{array} \right\}$$

In this context, zero is neither positive nor negative.

Simple conditionals of the first type can be connected together for greater convenience by the logical operators *AND* and *OR NOT*. (It will be observed that *AND* here is italicized: it is no longer an optional connector as it was in the sentence *ADD* W, X, AND Y *GIVING* Z.) Such a combination is known as a *compound condition*. If *AND* is the only logical operator used, then each condition in the compound condition must be true. In the following sentence:

IF Q *GREATER* THAN BALANCE *AND* CODE *EQUALS* 10
    GO TO ORDER.

the program would go to the paragraph labelled ORDER only if both conditions were true.

If *OR* is the only logical connector used, then just one of the connected conditions has to be true if the program is to obey the rest of the sentence.

It will have been noticed that *NOT* has been used already in the various formats of the *IF* statement, enclosed in square brackets as an option.

To economize on writing, an implied subject can be used in these compound conditional statements. Instead of writing

IF CODE *EQUALS* 2 *OR* CODE *EQUALS* 4 *OR* CODE *EQUALS* 7

the programmer could write

IF CODE *EQUALS* 2 *OR* 4 *OR* 7.

This naturally can only be done when each simple condition has the same subject and relation.

If, as in the above example, the logical operators are identical the statement could be condensed to

IF CODE *EQUALS* 2, 4, *OR* 7.

8

If both *AND* and *OR* occur in a compound condition, *AND* takes precedence. Parentheses can be used to override this. When in doubt as to the order of evaluation of the truth value of a compound condition, parentheses should be used. If $X = 1$, $Y = 2$ and $Z = 7$, the condition

X *EQUALS* 1 *OR* Y *EQUALS* 2 *AND* Z *EQUALS* 4

would have the value true, and the condition

(X *EQUALS* 1 *OR* Y *EQUALS* 2) *AND* Z *EQUALS* 4

would have the value false.

There is an alternative form of the *IF* statement that prescribes action to be taken when the condition is false as well as when it is true. The form is

IF condition

$$\left\{ \begin{array}{l} \text{statement-1} \\ \textit{NEXT SENTENCE} \end{array} \right\} \left\{ \begin{array}{l} \textit{ELSE} \\ \textit{OTHERWISE} \end{array} \right\} \left\{ \begin{array}{l} \text{statement-2} \\ \textit{NEXT SENTENCE} \end{array} \right\}.$$

Statement-1 may be a simple statement or a series of simple statements separated by AND, comma or semi-colon (compound statement). Statement-2 may be simple, compound or another conditional statement. If the condition is true, the statement after the condition is executed or the program goes to the beginning of the *NEXT SENTENCE*. If the condition is false, the statement before *ELSE* is omitted and the program either obeys the statement after the *ELSE* or goes to the beginning of the *NEXT SENTENCE*.

Programs can be complicated if the statement after ELSE is another conditional statement, for example,

IF I IS *LESS* THAN N *ADD* 1 *TO* I AND *GO TO* RENEW
ELSE IF I *EQUALS* J *GO TO* REPLENISH
ELSE GO TO ERROR-PRINT.

Beginners should, as far as possible, avoid constructions like this.

The words *ELSE NEXT SENTENCE* can be omitted if they are the last words in a sentence. If *NEXT SENTENCE* occurs as the last sentence of the last paragraph of a group being performed, the next sentence being obeyed depends on the *PERFORM* verb (this will become clear after the section on *Subroutines*.

If it is desired to add explanatory comments to a program the *NOTE* verb should be used. This will not be compiled into object program code and is merely to help comprehension of the program. Examples could be

NOTE END OF TAX ROUTINE.
NOTE THIS SECTION IS ONLY USED FOR EXPORT
ORDERS.

If *NOTE* occurs as the first word of a paragraph the whole paragraph will be treated as notes. If it is not the first word of a paragraph the commentary ends with the first full stop followed by a space.

Input/Output

Before any processing can be done on any input or output file it must be 'opened'. In the case of magnetic-tape files, this involves the checking of tape labels. The form is

> *OPEN INPUT* file-name 1 ,file-name 2 ...,
> *OUTPUT* file-name 3 ,file-name 4 ....

It is important to remember that no reading of data records is done by the *OPEN* verb. Examples of its use could be

> *OPEN INPUT* STOCK-A, RECEIPTS, *OUTPUT* STOCK-B,
> ORDERS.
> *OPEN INPUT* PAY-RECORDS.

When the processing of information in a file is completed, certain operations are performed that vary from one compiler to another. It is usual with magnetic-tape files to perform certain label operations. The *CLOSE* verb must be used. The form is

> *CLOSE* file-name 1 [*NO REWIND*] [,file-name 2 ...].
> *CLOSE* LEDGER-MARCH *NO REWIND*.
> *CLOSE* TRANS, RECEIPTS, STOCK-A, STOCK-B.

If the information in the file is recorded on magnetic tape, the tape is rewound unless the *NO REWIND* option is used.

Some compilers have special conventions for handling such situations as multireel files.

The *READ* verb reads the next record from a file into the area specified for the record in the data division. The form of the statement is

> *READ* file-name RECORD [*INTO* data-name] AT *END*
> imperative statement.

This verb makes the next record available. If the file contains more than one type of record, the programmer should make a test as to which record has been read. If there are no more records in the file, the program obeys the statement after *END*.

The *INTO* option must be used only if the file contains only one record (level 1 data-name). The option behaves as if it were taken into the data-name by the *MOVE* verb. If the *BLOCK* option is used (see the earlier section on *Data Division*), the *READ* verb automatically handles all data manipulations associated with the end of a block. Examples of the *READ* statement could be

READ RECEIPTS AT *END CLOSE* RECEIPTS *GO TO* PHASE 2.
READ STOCK-A AT *END GO TO* FINISH.

For output files, the *WRITE* verb writes a record to a magnetic file, prints it or punches it. The form is

WRITE record-name [*FROM* data-name 1]

$$\left[\left\{ \begin{array}{l} BEFORE \\ AFTER \end{array} \right\} \text{ADVANCING} \left\{ \begin{array}{l} \text{data-name 2} \\ \text{integer} \\ \text{mnemonic name} \end{array} \right\} \begin{array}{l} \text{LINES} \\ \text{LINES} \end{array} \right]$$

This verb writes a record, and if records are blocked appropriate action is automatically taken. After *WRITE* has been used the record named is no longer available.

The statement

WRITE X *FROM* Y

has the same meaning as

MOVE Y *TO* X   *WRITE* X.

No line spacing takes place if the ADVANCING option is not used, and the printing starts at position 1 on a new line. The ADVANCING option is normally used; mnemonic names like PAGE vary from one compiler to another. If *BEFORE* is used, the record is printed before line spacing occurs. When *AFTER* is used, line spacing occurs before the record is printed. If we wish to halt the program to receive small amounts of data from the console typewriter we use the *ACCEPT* verb. The form is

ACCEPT data-name   *FROM* mnemonic name.

If the *FROM* option is not used, data are received from a standard input unit specified for each compiler. The mnemonic name is specified in the environment division to refer to a particular peripheral device.

DISPLAY is used for the output of small amounts of data on the console typewriter. The form is

$$\text{DISPLAY} \left\{ \begin{array}{l} \text{data-name 1} \\ \text{literal 1} \end{array} \right\} \left[\left\{ \begin{array}{l} \text{,data-name 2} \\ \text{,literal 2} \end{array} \right\} ... \right] \begin{array}{l} UPON \text{ mnemonic} \\ \text{name.} \end{array}$$

The mnemonic names are defined in the environment division. In some compilers they can be omitted and then a standard output peripheral device is used.

Subroutines

We often need to use common sequences of instructions at various points in a program. The idea of a subroutine was demonstrated in chapter 2. In Cobol, entrance to a subroutine is effected by the *PERFORM* verb. There are many options of this verb. The form of the simplest is

PERFORM procedure-name 1 [*THRU* procedure-name 2.]

A simple example could be

PERFORM CASH-ROUTINE.

In this example the program would go to the paragraph headed CASH-ROUTINE, would obey all that paragraph and then return to the statement following the *PERFORM* statement.

The following program outline will demonstrate the action of the *PERFORM* verb.

> *ADD* A *TO* B.
> *PERFORM* CASH-ROUTINE.
> *ADD* X *TO* Y.
> ... ...
> ... ...
> ... ...
> CASH-ROUTINE.
> ... ...
> ... ...

The program would go to the paragraph headed CASH-ROUTINE after obeying *ADD* A *TO* B. After completing execution of all the statements in the paragraph, it would return to the statement after the *PERFORM* verb, *ADD* X *TO* Y.

When it is desired to obey more than one paragraph before returning to the statement after the *PERFORM* verb, the *THRU* option must be used. There can be any number of paragraphs between procedure-name 1 and procedure-name 2. The following outline will illustrate the action of the *THRU* option.

> *ADD* A *TO* B.
> *PERFORM* CASH-ROUTINE *THRU* TIME.
> *ADD* X *TO* Y.
> ... ...
> ... ...
> ... ...
> ... ...

CASH-ROUTINE.

... ...

... ...

AUDIT.

... ...

... ...

PRINTOUT.

... ...

... ...

TIME.

... ...

... ...

WAGE-CHECK.

... ...

... ...

The program would go to the paragraph headed CASH-ROUTINE after the statement *ADD* A *TO* B. The paragraphs headed CASH-ROUTINE, AUDIT, PRINTOUT and TIME would be obeyed, and the program would return to the statement *ADD* X *TO* Y after obeying the final statement of the paragraph headed TIME.

The last sentence of a paragraph that should return to the statement after a *PERFORM* verb should not contain a *GO* verb. No *GO* verb should be present in the last sentence of the paragraph headed CASH-ROUTINE in the first example, and in the last sentence of the paragraph headed TIME in the second example.

These are the simplest options of the *PERFORM* verb. There are many useful variations, which are not, however, found in all compilers. The appropriate Cobol programming manual should be consulted for details of these.

PL/I

PL/I was developed by IBM in conjunction with SHARE and GUIDE, two groups of users of large-scale IBM computers. The six objectives of the language can be summarized as follows:

1. Any combination of symbols having a clear and unambiguous meaning should be allowed.
2. It should never be necessary to use machine language or assembly language in a program because of some deficiency in the high-level language.
3. The language should be as far as possible independent of any particular computer.
4. The language should be 'modular' so that many different combinations of features can be chosen for different uses.
5. It should cater for the beginner by allowing him initially to learn only the notation most natural and useful to him.
6. It should be a programming language with a syntax that makes listing readable and easy to write and punch.

PL/I aims to break down the barriers between commercial and scientific high-level languages since many commercial programs now use operational-research techniques involving mathematical programming. The expanded output facilities are of use to the scientific programmer in preparing reports.

"Catering for the novice" is one of the most attractive features of the language. A programmer can use the language at his own level of experience and need not know the most sophisticated features of PL/I. Every option has been given a 'default' interpretation that would be the one most useful to a programmer who was ignorant of the existence of the option.

The treatment of PL/I in this chapter deals with the features of the language likely to be of most use to a beginner who does not have access to a large computer. To gain an idea of the full power and utility of the language, reference should be made to the appropriate IBM Reference Manuals.† These will illustrate the attractiveness of the features of PL/I that are not mentioned here. It will be seen that the superior features of both scientific and commercial programming languages have been incorporated.

† IBM System/360 PL/I Reference Manual, Form C–28–8201; IBM System/360, PL/I Subset Reference Manual, Form C–28–8202.

Character set

Either a 60 character set or a 48 character set may be used for a PL/I program depending on the punching equipment available. This chapter will use the 60 character set which consists of:

A – Z		,
0–9		.
$	(currency symbol)	'
@		%
#	(number sign)	;
blank		:
=		¬ (not)
+		& (and)
–		| (or)
*		>
/		<
(		— (break character
)		(used as shown here))
' (or ")		?
||		

Program statements can be written in a free-field format. The instructions in a PL/I program are known as *statements*, and a statement can be regarded as a meaningful string of characters *always* terminated by a semi-colon.

Variable names

It will be remembered from chapter 3 that one of the essential features of a high-level programming language is the facility to name units of the computer store by names meaningful to the programmer such as TAX, SQUARE, ROOT.

Variable names in PL/I form part of the class of *identifiers*. An identifier is a combination of letters, numbers and break characters and must begin with a letter and be not more than 31 characters long (the characters $, @ and # are considered as letters). Examples of acceptable identifiers are:

TAX   SHEENA   SQUARE1   BOND007   @47   NET_PRICE

An identifier must *not* contain blanks. A blank ends an identifier.

Variable declarations

Beginners need not declare variables holding numerical values. If the first character of a name is in the range I–N, the variable will contain an integer held in fixed-point form. If the first character of a name is any other letter, the name will contain a real number held in floating-point form. The precision to which each kind of number is held is determined by the computer used.

It is more usual, however, to use a DECLARE statement. The general form of the statement is

DECLARE *name attributes*;

where *name* is a variable identifier and *attributes* describe its characteristics. Usually several variables of the same type are declared together. In that case the attributes are 'factored' and the general form of such a statement is

DECLARE (*name-1, name-2, ...*) *attributes*;

If a variable is to be held in fixed point form, it is declared in the following format:

DECLARE *name* FIXED(p, q);

p is the number of digits in the item and q is the number of decimal places. p is known as the precision attribute. An example could be

DECLARE AMOUNT FIXED(4, 2);

which would have two digits before the decimal point and two digits after the point.

When declaring an integer the number of decimal places need not be stated, for example,

DECLARE WHOLE—NUMBER FIXED(4);

It is not even necessary in declaring integers to specify the number of digits, as this would be determined by the particular computer used so that the above statement could have been written

DECLARE WHOLE—NUMBER FIXED;

If several integers are declared together the form would be

DECLARE(I, J, H, N, S) FIXED;

If it is desired to use numbers in floating-point form a typical declaration would be

DECLARE REAL—NUMBER FLOAT;

The number of digits required can be specified in parentheses, but if it is omitted the number of digits would be determined by the particular computer used. If it was desired to have ten digits in the above example the declaration would read

DECLARE REAL—NUMBER FLOAT(10);

FLOAT and FIXED are known as scale attributes.

The form of arithmetic data items can also be declared by the use of the PICTURE attribute, which gives a symbolic representation or 'picture' of the contents of the variable. The general form of this type of declaration is

DECLARE name PICTURE 'specifications';

where specifications is a string of characters enclosed in primes.

The character 9 specifies that the corresponding digit position in the item will contain a decimal digit. The character V denotes the position of the assumed decimal point so that

DECLARE SUM FIXED(5);

is equivalent to

DECLARE SUM PICTURE '99999';

and

DECLARE TOTAL FIXED(5, 1);

is equivalent to

DECLARE TOTAL PICTURE '9999V9';

The character F can be used with an integer following it in parentheses to indicate the number of places the decimal point should be shifted to the right (a negative number specifies a shift to the left). The following declarations are equivalent:

DECLARE AMOUNT PICTURE '999V99';
DECLARE AMOUNT PICTURE '99999F(−2)';
DECLARE AMOUNT PICTURE 'V99999F(3)';

A repetition factor saves writing in using the PICTURE specification. It is an integer enclosed in parentheses preceding the PICTURE character that is to be repeated so that the following declarations are equivalent:

DECLARE SUM PICTURE '99999';
DECLARE SUM PICTURE '(5)9';

Sometimes it is desired to store some characters, such as the letters of a name, in a variable. Such a group of characters is called a 'string'. Character strings have two attributes: CHARACTER, which specifies a character string, and a length attribute, which specifies the number of characters in the string.

DECLARE NAME CHARACTER(4);

is a typical use of a character declaration.

Invariably character data such as names or addresses will not be the same length for each name or address with which the program has to deal. In such a case the VARYING attributes may be used. If so, the length attribute specifies the maximum length of the string. The following statement illustrates a typical use of this attribute:

DECLARE(NAME,ADDRESS) CHARACTER(15) VARYING;

Both NAME and ADDRESS here are variable-length character strings with a maximum length of 15 characters.

Constants

There are various forms of constant; the following are those most useful to a beginner.

A decimal fixed-point constant contains one or more decimal digits and an optional decimal point and sign. If no decimal point is included, it is assumed that the constant is a decimal integer. Examples of such constants are:

37.198   .87   +234.   −192

A decimal floating-point constant is represented by one or more decimal digits with an optional decimal point followed by the letter E followed by an optionally signed decimal exponent.

3.E2   is   300.
−3.1E−2   is   −.031

The following constants have all the same value:

1.23E−2   12.3E−3   .0123E0   .0000123E3

A character string constant is represented as one or more characters enclosed in primes, for example,

'COMPUTATION'

Blanks are significant in a character string and are considered as characters like any other so that the string

'JULIA IS MARVELLOUS'

contains 19 characters and includes two blank spaces.

Arithmetic expressions

Arithmetic expressions are composed of operators, operands (identifiers and constants) and brackets.

The operators are:

+   addition   −   subtraction or negation
*   multiplication   /   division
**   exponentiation.

Typical arithmetic expressions are

$$A/B+3 * D, \quad E ** (4-X)+9 * G$$

The priority of operations is exponentiation, then multiplication and division, and lastly addition and subtraction. Subject to this, the left-hand operation is done first for addition and subtraction and the right-hand operation for exponentiation and negation so that

$$X-Y*Z \quad \text{means} \quad X-(Y*Z)$$

and

$$X ** A ** B \quad \text{means} \quad X ** (A ** B)$$

Plain parentheses can be used to change the order in which operations are performed so that the first example above could be rewritten as

$$(X-Y)*Z$$

to obtain another meaning. Brackets should be added whenever a programmer is doubtful of the wisdom of their omission; redundant brackets are ignored by the compiler.

Functions are provided in PL/I to perform operations in common use such as the computation of square roots and logarithms.

There are many built-in functions in the language and a selection is given below. Function values have the same base, scale and precision as their argument, which in the following examples can be an arithmetic expression.

ABS(X)	the absolute value
CEIL(X)	the smallest integer greater than or equal to the argument; e.g. if $X = CEIL(-3.4)$ then X will contain -3
FLOOR(X)	the largest integer less than or equal to the argument; e.g. if $X = FLOOR(3.4)$ then X will contain 3
COS(X)	cosine of X radians
SIN(X)	sine of X radians
TAN(X)	tangent of X radians

EXP(X)	e^X
LOG(X)	natural logarithm of X
LOG10(X)	$\log_{10} X$
ATAN(X)	the value of the inverse tangent of X so that the value returned is in the range $-\pi/2$ to $\pi/2$
TRUNC(X)	X truncated to an integer TRUNC(1.6) is 1; TRUNC(−6.9) is −6
MAX(X1, X2, ...)	the maximum value of an arbitrary number of arguments; e.g. A = 4; B = 1; C = 2; D = −6; E = MAX(A, B, C, D); E will contain 4
MIN(X1, X2, ...)	the minimum value of an arbitrary number of arguments. Using the variable values of the above example, F = MIN(A, B, C, D); F will contain −6

Assignment statements

The assignment statement has the general form

variable = *expression*;

Typical assignment statements would be

X = −3.2;
Y = Z+LOG(P+T);
P = P+1;

The = does *not* denote equality (as Fortran and EMA programmers will realize!). The value of the arithmetic expression on the right-hand side is evaluated, and the result is placed in the variable name on the left-hand side.

Characters can be inserted in a string variable by means of the assignment statement, for example,

SHEENA = 'WONDERFUL';

The characters are left-justified within the variable so that if the variable has more character positions than the expression on the right-hand side of the assignment statement it is filled out to the right with blanks. If the variable has been declared with less character positions than the right-hand side expression, the string in the expression is truncated on the right.

In the section of program:

DECLARE JULIA CHARACTER(6);
JULIA = 'WONDERFUL';

the variable would contain 'WONDER' and the three characters on the right would be dropped. We sometimes need to assign the same value to more than one variable. If so, a multiple assignment statement is used. The general form of the multiple assignment statement is

variable-1, *variable*-2, ..., *variable*-n = *expression*.

The statement

P, Q, A = 45;

would insert the value 45 in P, Q and A.

A statement may be labelled if we want to refer it to at another point in the program. Labels are constructed according to the general rules for the construction of identifiers shown in the earlier section on *Variable Names*. A label is connected by a colon to the statement to which it refers. A typical example of a labelled statement could be

START: X, Y = 0;

The identifier used for a label must not be the same as that used for a variable. The use of labels will become clear when the GO TO statement is mentioned.

Initialization

Variables can be set to initial values by using the INITIAL attribute in the declare statement rather than by writing separate assignment statements. The general form is

DECLARE *name attributes* INITIAL (*value*);

where *value* is a constant of the appropriate data type. A typical example would be

DECLARE E FIXED INITIAL(1);

which would set the variable E to the starting value of 1. If the insertion of starting values is accomplished by the INITIAL attribute, the initial values with which a program is working can easily be perceived.

Comment

We sometimes wish to insert comments in a program to explain a step to the reader. A comment can be inserted whenever a blank is allowed (except in a character-string constant). The form of a comment is a character string preceded by /* and followed by */, for example,

/* CLEARS COUNTERS */

Naturally the comment must not contain the terminating sequence */.
If a program is used by many people, comments should be freely inserted even if the programmer is punching his own program!

Transfer of control and conditional statements

A program is obeyed statement by statement unless control is transferred to another part of the program.

If it is desired to break the sequence of statements and resume the program at a labelled statement, the GO TO statement is used. The general form is

GO TO *label*;

and a typical example could be

GO TO START;

A GO TO statement may transfer control 'forwards' or 'backwards' within a program.

An important facility of a digital computer is the power to transfer control to various parts of the computer according to a decision taken by the program. In chapter 2 these were the steps that were written in a diamond-shaped box.

One way of accomplishing this in PL/I is by a simple IF statement. The general form is:

IF *condition* THEN *statement*;

An example could be

IF Y = 1 THEN GO TO RESTORE;

If the condition is untrue, the statement following THEN is skipped and the program obeys the next statement. In the following sequences of instructions:

IF Y = 1 THEN Y = 7; Y = Y + 1;

if Y is equal to 1 the statement after THEN and the following statement are obeyed, so that at the end of the two statements Y has the value 8. If, however, Y had the initial value of 4, the statement after THEN would be omitted and Y would have the value 5. It must be observed here that the = sign really means equals (unlike its use in the assignment statement).

= is an example of a comparison operator. In the 60-character set the comparison operators are:

=	equal	$> =$	greater than or equal
$\neg =$	not equal to	$<$	less than
$>$	greater than	$\neg <$	not less than
$\neg >$	not greater than	$< =$	less than or equal to

Simple conditions can be combined by utilizing the logical operators listed below:

$$\neg \quad \text{not}$$
$$\& \quad \text{and}$$
$$| \quad \text{or}$$

In the following example, the statement after THEN is only executed if I $=2$ and J $=7$:

IF I $= 2$ & J $= 7$ THEN *statement*;

If it were desired to execute the statement if either of the above conditions (or both) were true, the 'or' logical operator would be used:

IF I $= 2 | $ J $= 7$ THEN *statement*;

The hierarchy of the logical operators is 'not', 'and', 'or'. Parentheses may be used to override this sequence.

We sometimes need to perform one of two alternative statements according to the truth or falsity of the condition. The form of the IF statement used then is

IF *condition* THEN *statement-1*;
ELSE *statement-2*;
next statement;

The following sequence of statements puts the larger of two numbers contained in I and J in LARGE.

IF I $>$ J THEN   LARGE $=$ I;
            ELSE   LARGE $=$ J;

IF can follow an ELSE, so that complicated constructions are possible. The following example places the largest of three numbers contained in I, J and K in LARGE.

IF I $>$ J & I $>$ K   THEN LARGE $=$ I;
ELSE IF J $>$ K   THEN LARGE $=$ J;
            ELSE LARGE $=$ K;

Labyrinthine sets of conditional statements are feasible but should be avoided by beginners.

So far only a single statement has been executed after the THEN or ELSE. Often it is convenient to execute a group of statements. The facility for doing this is the DO group.
The general form is

DO;
statement-1;
statement-2;
...;
statement-n;
END;

The DO statement, the END statement and the statements between these comprise the DO group.
The following sequence of statements utilizes DO groups to put the larger of two numbers contained in I and J in LARGE and the smaller in LEAST.

IF I > J THEN
DO;
    LARGE = I;
    LEAST = J;
END;
    ELSE
DO;
    LARGE = J;
    LEAST = I;
END;

The END statements here do not terminate the program (for procedure see a later section). Each DO group must have its own END statement.

List-directed input and output

To enable the beginner to write some realistic sections of program, it is necessary to mention input and output facilities so that data may be read and results printed. List-directed input/output is perhaps the simplest.
In this form of input, items to be read are separated by one or more blanks or a comma.
The program statement to read the items of data has the general form

GET LIST (*list*);

list is a sequence of variables separated by commas.

9

In the sequence of instructions

```
DECLARE A        FIXED(3, 2),
        I        FIXED(4),
        NAME     CHARACTER(6);
GET LIST (A, I, NAME);
```

with the following data

1.76,   −75,   'SHEENA',   −2.34,   192,   'JULIA'

the first time the GET statement is obeyed A will contain 1.76, I will contain −75 and NAME will be set to the character string SHEENA. If the GET statement is executed a second time, A will contain −2.34, I will contain 192 and NAME will have the character string JULIA.

If the list on a GET LIST statement contains n variables, n items will be taken from the data list each time GET LIST is obeyed (there is an exception for an array; see the next section on *Subscripted Variables*.

An output list may contain arithmetic expressions and constants as well as variable names. Constants are printed in the form they appear in the list of a PUT LIST statement, and variables are printed according to their attributes.

The following sequence of statements:

```
DECLARE A FIXED(5, 2);
A = −3.4;
PUT LIST ('A = ', A)
```

would print

A = −3.40

If it is desired to move to a new line, SKIP should be inserted after the parenthesis. This is discussed in greater detail later.

A complete program will now be shown. It is desired to print numbers between 1 and 100 with their squares and cubes.

```
TITLE:   PROCEDURE OPTIONS (MAIN);

         I = 1;
START:   J = I * I;
         PUT LIST (I, J, I * J) SKIP;
         I = I * I;
         IF I < 101 THEN GO TO START;
         STOP; END;
```

Each program must commence with an identifier followed by a colon and PROCEDURE OPTIONS (MAIN) and must terminate with END;

Exercises 7.1†

1. Print the integers 1–100 with their square, cube, square root and cube root.
2. Compute and print the reciprocals of the numbers 2–100 to six decimal places.
3. Read 12 sales amounts for the 12 months and print each as a ratio to January with January $= 100$.
4. Read ten pairs of numbers representing the smaller sides of ten right-angled triangles and print the ten values of the hypotenuse.
5. Print a table of circles with areas increasing in steps of a square metre from 1 to 100 square metres, and their corresponding radii (assume $\pi = 3.14$).
6. $\pi/4 = 1 - \frac{1}{3} + \frac{1}{5} - \frac{1}{7} + \frac{1}{9} \ldots$
   Evaluate 1000 terms of this series and print out the value of π to eight decimal places every 100 terms.
7. Compute and print the terms of the Fibonacci series ($x_{n+1} = x_n + x_{n-1}$) between 10^5 and 10^8. The first few terms are 0 1 1 2 3 5 8 ....
8. The solution of the simultaneous equations

   $$ax + by + c = 0$$
   $$px + qy + r = 0$$

   is given by

   $$x = (br - cq)/(aq - bp)$$
   $$y = (pc - ar)/(aq - bp)$$

   Read a, b, c, p, q, r and compute and print x and y.
   Print INDETERMINATE if $aq - bp = 0$.
   Print NOT INDEPENDENT if $a/p = b/q = c/r$.

Subscripted variables

It is often necessary to perform operations on tables, matrices and similar groups of like variables. In PL/I such a group is referred to as an array.

An array is declared with a dimension attribute. The following example

DECLARE K(100) FIXED(4);

declares a one-dimensional array K of 100 members. Each member of the array has the attribute FIXED(4). The first element here is K(1) and the last is K(100).

The general form of an array declaration is:

DECLARE *name* (*dimension*) *other attributes*;

† Suggested solutions to all exercises follow after chapter 8.

In the case of the array declared above, each member would be referenced by a subscript containing a value in the range 1–100 so that the statement

K(45) = 17;

would refer to the forty-fifth member of the array.

In arrays declared in the above manner it is assumed that the first member of the array has a subscript of 1. This subscript is often referred to as the *lower bound* and the highest subscript (100 in this example) as the *upper bound*.

Both bounds can be specified in some compilers, for example,

DECLARE K(0: 99) FIXED(4);

The first element here is K(0) and the last is K(99).

The upper bound must be greater than or equal to the lower bound; either or both can be negative. A subscript can be any expression that is evaluated and converted to an integer. A subscript must fall within the bounds of the array.

It is sometimes essential to use a matrix or a table in which the elements are considered as forming rows and columns so that a two-dimensional array is required in the program. The appropriate array declaration for a table with three rows and four columns is

DECLARE TABLE (3, 4);

The lower bound for both dimensions is assumed to be one. Lower as well as upper bounds maybe specified for either or both dimensions. Arrays may have up to 32 dimensions in PL/I; more than two are rarely required.

The INITIAL attribute may be used to specify the initial value of the elements of an array. The values specified by this attribute give starting values to a corresponding number of array elements. The statement

DECLARE K(8) FIXED INITIAL (1, 7, 0, −9);

would set the first four elements of the array K to 1, 7, 0 and −9 respectively. The values of the remaining four elements are undefined. An iteration factor can be used in the specification of initial values for an array. In the following example the entire array is set to 0:

DECLARE M(100) INITIAL ((100) 0);

More than one iteration factor can be used in the following example:

DECLARE N(8) INITIAL ((2) 0, (4) 1);

The first two elements are set to 0, the next four to 1 and the values of the last two are undefined.

When multi-dimensional arrays are initialized, operations are performed so that the right-hand subscript is varied most rapidly and the left-hand subscript least rapidly. The statement

DECLARE L(2, 3) FIXED INITIAL (7, 8, 9, 10, 11, 12);

would place the following values in L:

$$L(1, 1) = 7 \quad L(1, 2) = 8 \quad L(1, 3) = 9$$
$$L(2, 1) = 10 \quad L(2, 2) = 11 \quad L(2, 3) = 12$$

Input or output of an entire array can be accomplished by putting the array name in an input or output list. The whole array in the previous example could be printed in the same order (row by row) by the statement

PUT LIST (L);

Under certain conditions unsubscripted array names may be used to form array expressions. If arrays K and L have the same number of dimensions and the same subscript bounds, each element in the array L could be given the value of three times the corresponding element in the array K by the statement

$$L = 3 * K;$$

Therefore arrays of identical size and dimension can be used in the same way as simple variables. The following example puts the sum of two arrays into a third array:

DECLARE (J(2, 3), K(2, 3), L(2, 3)) FIXED;
GET LIST (J, K);
$$L = J + K;$$

The statement

$$K = K + 1;$$

for an array K adds one to each element of the array.

DO statements

The DO group was encountered in the section on *Transfer of Control and Conditional Statements* for grouping statements after THEN or ELSE. The DO statement can also be used to specify that statements between DO and the corresponding END are to be executed a certain number of times. This is a very powerful feature of PL/I and provides a more economic method of writing program loops than using a conditional statement to return to the start of the loop.

Perhaps the most useful form of the DO loop is

DO *variable* = *expression1* BY *expression2* TO *expression3*;

The loop is initially obeyed to the appropriate END statement with the variable taking the value of *expression1*, then on each subsequent pass being incremented by *expression 2* until the value exceeds the value of *expression3*. (If *expression2* is negative, the variable is decremented until its value is less than *expression3*.)

The sequence of statements to print numbers between 1 and 100 with their squares and cubes shown on page 122 can be rewritten with a DO loop as follows:

```
DO I = 1 BY 1 TO 100;
J = I * I;
PUT LIST (I, J, I * J);
END;
```

If *expression2* is 1 the BY *expression2* may be omitted so that the DO statement in the above example may be rewritten

DO I = 1 TO 100;

Another form of DO loop is

DO *variable* = *expression1*, *expression2*, ..., *expression n*;

This sets the variable (in a DO loop often referred to as the control variable) to the value of each of the expressions in turn.

The DO loop used in the above example can also be written with the form

DO *variable* = *expression1* TO *expression3* BY *expression2*;

Another form of the DO loop is

DO WHILE (*condition*);

This requires the statements in the loop to be repeated as long as the *condition* (which is evaluated before each pass through the loop) is true.

The sequence of statements to print the squares and cubes between 1 and 100 could be rewritten as

```
I = 0;
DO WHILE (I < 100);
I = I + 1;
J = I * I;
PUT LIST (I, J, I * J);
END;
```

BY and WHILE can be combined so that the above sequence could be written as

DO I = 1 BY 1 WHILE (I < 101);
J = I * I;
PUT LIST (I, J, I * J);
END;

There is also a form:

DO *variable* = *expression1* BY *expression2* TO *expression3*
WHILE *condition*;

The loop is obeyed (if *expression2* is positive) until either *variable* > *expression3* or *condition* is false.

The expressions in the specifications at the start of a DO loop are evaluated when the loop is first entered. Thus they cannot be effectively changed by any statement within the range of the DO loop. The control variable can, however, be altered, and if such an alteration takes its value outside the specified range the loop will not be repeated. Such an alteration of the control variable is best avoided.

A GO TO statement may lead from a DO loop to a point outside the loop. It is very important to emphasize that a GO TO statement outside a DO loop may *not* transfer to a point within a repetitive DO loop since the setting of the initial values of the expressions would be bypassed. Unlike similar constructions in Algol and Fortran the PL/I DO loop defines the value of the control variable when the loop is terminated normally. The value is the first one that fails to meet the conditions for execution of the loop, so that in the above example I would have the value 101 on exit from the loop.

DO loops can occur within a DO loop. Such a construction is referred to as a 'nest' of DO loops. The only restriction is that the inner DO loop must be completely within the range of the outer one, so that the END corresponding to an inner DO must appear before an END corresponding to the next outer DO.

The following example sums the elements of a matrix with ten rows and ten columns and illustrates the nested construction.

```
        SUM = 0;
L1;     DO I = 1 BY 1 TO 10;
L2;     DO J = 1 BY 1 TO 10;
        SUM = SUM + M(I, J);
        END L2;
        END L1;
```

It will be observed that to facilitate identification of DOs and ENDs each matching DO and END has been labelled.

If a label is used following an END statement, the compiler interprets each END statement as corresponding to the DO statement having the same label as well as all DO statements within its scope, so that the above example could be rewritten as

```
     SUM = 0;
L1;  DO I = 1 BY 1 TO 10;
     DO J = 1 BY 1 TO 10;
     SUM = SUM + M(I, J);
     END L1;
```

The END statement terminates both DO loops since the label, L1, is the same as the label on the outermost DO statement.

A DO loop can contain all three of the forms so that in the following sequence:

```
DO K = 1, 3, 5 BY 1 TO 8, 10 BY 3 WHILE (I < = 19), 25;
PUT LIST (I);
END;
```

the value of I to be printed would be:

1   3   5   6   7   8   10   13   16   19   25

Exercises 7.2
Do questions 1–6 of Exercises 7.1 using DO loops.

Procedures
A procedure in PL/I is a set of statements: simple programs consist of a single procedure whereas others may use subroutines (see chapter 2). In that case each subroutine will also be considered as a procedure. Every program must therefore contain at least one procedure. All procedures have a title followed by a colon, and the main program has PROCEDURE OPTIONS (MAIN) written after it. Therefore the complete program for printing the squares and cubes of numbers between 1 and 100 could be

```
POWERS: PROCEDURE OPTIONS (MAIN);
DO I = 1 TO 100;
J = I * I;
PUT LIST (I, J, I * J);
END;
STOP; END POWERS;
```

The PROCEDURE statement of a subroutine usually contains the parameters in which are placed values taken from the section of program calling procedure. A typical procedure for converting millimetres to centimetres and metres could be

```
        METRIC: PROCEDURE (P, L, S, D);
        DECLARE (P, L, S, D) FIXED;
        L = (P/1000);
        S = P − (1000 * L);
        IF S = 0 THEN GO TO OUT;
        S = (S/100);
OUT:    D = P − (1000 * L + 10 * S);
        RETURN;
        END METRIC;
```

The RETURN statement signifies a RETURN to the section of program which called the procedure.

The names in parentheses in the procedure statement are known as parameters. Parameters have no relation to other identifiers of the same name outside the procedure.

Subroutines are invoked (or called) by the CALL statement which has the form:

CALL *procedure-name* (argument-list);

A CALL for the procedure METRIC could be

CALL METRIC (E, F, G, H);

The arguments have one-to-one correspondence with the parameters and they should have identical attributes.

In the above example, although valid values must be passed to the parameters L, S and D, their main purpose is to store computed results in the storage allocated to F, G and H respectively. Any change in the value of P, L, S or D is a change in value of the corresponding argument. An argument also can be an arithmetic expression or constant, in which case a 'dummy argument' is created to hold the value. Arrays can be used as arguments if the attributes of the arrays in the argument-list are identical to those of the corresponding parameters.

It is sometimes wanted to use a procedure name in an arithmetic expression in the same way as a built-in function such as SQRT is used. A procedure to accomplish this is known as a function procedure or function. The procedure-name itself takes on the value which it is desired to return to the calling section of the program. The following procedure ROOT calculates the value of $(a^3 + b^3)^{\frac{1}{2}}$

```
ROOT: PROCEDURE (A, B) FLOAT;
DECLARE (A, B) FLOAT;
RETURN (SQRT(A** 3 + B ** 3));
END;
```

The attribute in the procedure statement specifies the attribute of the quantity to be returned by the procedure. The RETURN statement in this type of procedure specifies the value that is to be returned to the calling section of program. If it is desired, a RETURN statement can be used in this way to return a value in the type of procedure previously discussed such as METRIC if it is invoked by a function reference. If no value is returned in the procedure name, the RETURN statement is redundant since subroutines return to the calling section of the program by obeying either a RETURN or END statement.

A typical call of a function such as ROOT could be:

$$G = D - ROOT(X, Y);$$

It is sometimes difficult to ensure that the arguments of a procedure have identical attributes to the parameters. The ENTRY attribute can be used to specify the attributes of parameters; the arguments will be converted whenever necessary. The general form of the ENTRY attribute as included in a DECLARE statement is

DECLARE *name* ENTRY (*attribute, attribute, ..., attribute*);

where *name* is a procedure name and *attribute* is the attribute of the parameter and the required attribute of the argument.

An ENTRY declaration for the procedure METRIC would be:

DECLARE METRIC ENTRY (FIXED, FIXED, FIXED, FIXED);

and would be included with the declarations for P, L, S and D.

When the parameter is an array the ENTRY statement can contain an asterisk for each dimension so that the statement

DECLARE JULIA ENTRY ((*, *) FIXED);

declares the procedure JULIA to have as its only parameter a two-dimensional fixed-point array with bounds identical to the bounds of the array used in the argument.

The RETURNS attribute specifies the attributes of the value returned by a function to the calling section of program. The ENTRY and RETURNS declaration for ROOT would be:

DECLARE ROOT ENTRY (FLOAT,FLOAT) RETURNS
(FLOAT);

It has already been stated that parameters do not have any relationship with any other identifier of the same name outside the procedure. However, identifiers other than parameters that do not appear in a DECLARE statement in a procedure are identical to identifiers of the same name inherited from a containing procedure. In the following example:

```
A1: PROCEDURE OPTIONS (MAIN);
DECLARE (V, W, X, Y) FIXED;
A2: PROCEDURE (X, A);
    DECLARE (X, A) FIXED;
    A = X+W;
    PUT LIST (A);
    END;
W = 8;
V = 5;
CALL A2 (V, Y);
END;
```

Y (which would be printed in A2) would have the value 13 as the W in A2 is identical to the W in A1 that was given the value of 8. W is said to be known in both A1 and A2. A is known only in A2 and cannot be referred to in A1 because its declaration is internal to A2.

The parameter X in A2 is distinct from the X in A1; each is known only in its respective procedure.

Further input/output facilities

Data-directed input/output

In this form of input the data file must contain the name of an identifier as well as the value that the identifier should hold. A typical item could be

$X = 7$.

If a program contained the statements

```
DECLARE A FLOAT,
        B FIXED,
        C CHARACTER(4);
        GET DATA;
```

and the input file contained

$B = 7$, $A = 8.4$, $C = 'LAMB'$; $C = 'GOAT'$;

the first execution of the GET statement would set A to 8.4, B to 7 and C to LAMB. If the statement is executed a second time C would be set to GOAT, and since the semi-colon terminates the execution of the statement, the values of A and B would be unaltered.

The GET DATA statement may be used with a *list* like the list used with list-directed input. The data file may assign values to any or all of the identifiers on the list and need not adhere to the order of the list.

In data-directed output the identifiers as well as their values are printed out in a form like

   M = 5678

The form is PUT DATA (*list*) like list-directed output. The list must contain only variable names, *not* constants or expressions. A semi-colon is printed after each execution of a PUT DATA statement.

Edit-directed input/output

In this form, every character is treated in accordance with a format specification. The statements have the form

   GET EDIT (*list*) (*format*);
   PUT EDIT (*list*) (*format*);

where *list* is the same as the list used for list-directed input/output and *format* is a series of format phrases that specify the form of the input/output data. The most common formats are considered below.

'A' format:

The phrase is A(n) where n is the number of characters that are treated as a character string. If n is omitted with an output format it is assumed to be the length of the item. If n is greater than the length of the item the item will be left-justified.

'X' format:

The phrase is X(n). On input the next n characters are ignored, and on output n blanks are inserted.

'F' format:

The phrase is F(n) or F(n, m). F(n) interprets on input the next n characters as a fixed-point integer, and on output prints n digits. If less than n digits are required, the number is right-justified. Leading zeros are replaced by blanks. The form F(n, m) assumes m digits to the right of the decimal point. If m is omitted no decimal point will be printed. If m is 0 the decimal point will be printed without any fractional part. It must be remembered that the decimal point occupies a digit position. It must also be borne in mind that a minus sign occupies a digit position so that the format phrase F(4) would deal with numbers in the range −999 to 9999.

The printing following the statements

   DECLARE   X CHARACTER(4)   INITIAL('LAMB'),
             Y FIXED   INITIAL(192),
             Z FLOAT   INITIAL(−2.3);
   PUT EDIT (X, Y, Z)(A(4), X(4), F(4), F(7, 2));

would be

   LAMB   192   −2.30

Format can be specified in a similar way to a PICTURE specification by means of a P format phrase. (This method will be familiar to Cobol programmers.) The general form of the P phrase is

P *'specifications'*

where 'specifications' consists of characters giving a 'picture' of the desired data representation. The most common specification characters are:

9 The corresponding character may be decimal digit
A The corresponding character may be an alphabetic character
X Any character may correspond to X
V A decimal point should be assumed at the corresponding point in the data item

The above characters may be used for both input and output specifications. The characters below are usually only used for output:

B A blank is to be inserted.
S A + or − is to be inserted at the corresponding point in the data item.
Z If the corresponding character is a leading zero it is to be replaced by a blank.
* This is like Z but replaces a leading zero by *.
+ If the associated item is positive or zero a plus sign will be inserted at the corresponding point in the output. If not, no sign will be printed.
− Same as above, except that − will only be inserted if the associated item is less than zero.
. A decimal point is to be inserted at the corresponding place in the data item.

The characters S, +, − can be 'floated' so that they will appear immediately to the left of the first non-blank character. Unauthorized characters cannot therefore be fraudulently inserted. The 'floating' is accomplished by writing the character in each position in which it is desired to 'float' it. The specification

P′ + + + +9′

could be used to print a value between +9999 and 0 with no space between + and the first digit printed.

Any format phrase may be preceded by a repetition factor that specifies the number of times the format phrase is to be repeated. The phrase

3 F(4)

specifies that three consecutive items are to be edited in accordance with the format phrase F(4).

Some general input/output facilities

Sometimes it is necessary to print the data read by a GET statement. If so, the COPY option can be used with a GET statement. The two forms are:

> GET COPY LIST (*list*);

or

> GET LIST (*list*) COPY;

This option can be used with all three types of input statement and prints the input data exactly as read without any alteration. Control over the printer is exercised by three options which may be used with PUT statements. The options are

> SKIP   or   SKIP(n)   (n is an integer)

This moves to a new line. If n is less than 1, printing will be resumed on the current line and any previous printed data on that line will be over-printed. If n = 1 the printing will take place on the next line. n after SKIP will give n − 1 blank lines if n > 0.

> LINE(n)   (n is an integer)

This specifies the particular line on which the next data item is to be printed.

> LINE(2)

This would move the paper to the second line of a page.

> PAGE

This starts a new page.

A PUT statement with an option may have no list so that the statement

> PUT PAGE;

will move to the start of a new page.

A printing option in the PUT statement specifies action to be taken by the printer before any items on the list are printed. The statement

> PUT PAGE LIST ('29 FEBRUARY 1968');

will print on the top of a new page

> 29 FEBRUARY 1968

In this section only a few of the many versatile input/output facilities have been discussed. The reader is referred to the appropriate programming manual for further details.

Block structure

A block is a collection of statements throughout which an identifier is established as a name. There are two kinds of blocks: procedure blocks and begin blocks. Procedure blocks have already been discussed under *Procedures* and can only be entered by means of a CALL statement or function reference.

A begin block has the general form

    BEGIN;
    Statement(s);
    END;

It is entered in the normal sequence of program execution. A begin block must be contained within another block, which may be another begin block or a procedure.

Identifiers declared within a block are internal to a block, and identifiers not declared within a containing block are known in the contained blocks. No attempt must be made to transfer to the interior of a block from a point outside it. We can, however, jump from an inner block to a point outside.

If the same identifier is used for a label in both an inner and outer block, the identifier in the outer block is 'masked out' during the execution of the statements in the inner block. In the following example:

    A: PROCEDURE OPTIONS (MAIN);
    ... ... ;
    B: G = H + V;
    ... ... ;
       BEGIN;
    ... ... ;
       B: W = X − Y;
    ... ... ;
       GO TO B;
    ... ... ;
       END;
    END;

The statement in the inner block GO TO B; would refer to label B in the inner block, and no reference could be made in the inner block to label B in the outer block.

Blocks enable a programmer to make efficient use of storage. The storage that is allocated upon entry to a block is freed upon exit so that this storage can be shared between several inner blocks on the same level. This facility can be very useful when several large arrays need to be declared at different stages in the program, since they can each be declared in parallel inner blocks and can share the same storage.

For production programs, various combinations of procedures can be used for different programs. A single MAIN procedure can call different compiled procedures to make up the program.

Data structures

The records used in commercial data processing have a hierarchical structure.

A *file* can contain one or more types of *record*, which contain *items* that often can be conveniently used in groups. The following example shows a hypothetical record (PAY-RECORD) that contains an employee code, name and pay-rates. The employee number consists of a departmental code prefixed to the individual employee code, so that 123456 could signify employee 456 in department 123. There are two pay-rates: normal and overtime.

```
PAY-RECORD
    EMPLOYEE NUMBER
        DEPT. NUMBER
        MAN NUMBER.
    NAME.
    PAY-RATES
        STANDARD RATE
        OVERTIME RATE.
```

In PL/I, data can be described in this hierarchical form by giving each item level numbers. Items are often referred to as levels. An example of this means of describing data could be:

```
DECLARE  1  PAY—RECORD,
            2  NUMBER,
                (3  DEPTCODE
                 3  MANCODE) FIXED,
            2  NAME CHARACTER(25),
            2  PAY—RATES,
                (3  NORMAL,
                 3  OVERTIME) FIXED;
```

The indentation is not obligatory but highlights the structure.

A PL/I structure must have only one level 1 item. Items which are not further subdivided are known as elementary levels: only elementary levels can have attributes. Each level name is separated from the following level number by a comma.

Brackets can be used to factor the FIXED attribute. The first attribute applies to the elementary levels DEPTCODE and MANCODE and the second to NORMAL and OVERTIME.

Structures can contain arrays, and a structure itself can be dimensioned as in the following example:

```
DECLARE   1   ABC(4),
              (2   D,
               2   E) FIXED;
```

The identifier D refers not to a single item but to four items: there is a D in each of the four elements of ABC. Reference to the particular D in ABC(3) would be accomplished by writing

ABC(3).D

This is known as a qualified name.

The following structures are identical except in their identifiers.

```
DECLARE   1   A,
              2   B FIXED,
              2   C,
              (3   D,
               3   E) FLOAT;
DECLARE   1   F,
              2   G FIXED,
              2   H,
              (3   I,
               3   J) FLOAT;
```

The expression

F = A;

would be legal and would transfer the elementary levels B, D and E into G, I and J respectively.

The expression

H = A;

would be illegal since these are not identical structures.

By using qualified names items can be moved from one structure to another, for example,

A.E = F.I;

The statement

H = 0;

would set both elements of the structure H to zero.

GET and PUT statements can deal with whole structures. The statement

GET LIST (A);

would read three data items into B, D and E.

10

Exercises 7.3

1. Read ten numbers, compute and print the average, and print the number with the greatest absolute deviation from the average.

2. Write a sequence of instructions to divide each element of a matrix with five rows and three columns by the largest element.

3. Write a section of program to print out the largest element of a matrix with three rows and four columns. It is also desired to print out the row and column of the largest element.

4. Print the prime numbers between 3 and 100.

5. Print a square with 19 rows and 19 columns with each of the rows and columns containing once only each of the numbers 1 to 19 (Latin square).

8
EXTENDED MERCURY AUTOCODE

Extended Mercury Autocode (EMA) is available for the ICL Atlas, Orion and 1900 series computers. There is a very large body of useful programs, such as the ICI sales forecasting routines, written in this language. Mercury autocode was originally written for the Ferranti Mercury computer. It was enthusiastically received and many dialects were rapidly developed. A modification of one such dialect, EXCHLF is a standard programming language for the University of London Institute of Computer Science.

Many useful extensions have been added to the original Mercury Autocode, and the ensuing version of the language, in which many important organizations write programs, is referred to as Extended Mercury Autocode.

Variables and indices

The reader is referred to the programming manual of his particular computer for details of program punching conventions on punched cards or punched paper tape.

Program statements are punched one per line. With one exception (see later, under *Printing*), spaces have no significance within a statement so that

A = B + C

is an acceptable form for

A = B + C

Capital or small letters or a mixture of both can be used so the following statements are equivalent

A = B + C
a = b + c
A = B + c

The store used by an EMA program for can most purposes be regarded as being composed of special variables, indices and main variables.

Special variables

Special variables are referred to by the letters

$$A-H \qquad U-\pi$$
$$A'-H' \qquad U'-\pi'$$

139

π follows Z in the EMA alphabet. The symbol $'$ is known as a 'prime' and A$'$ would be referred to as 'A primed'.

Special variables hold real numbers in floating-point form. The particular programming manual will give details as to the range and significance of a number held in a special variable.

Indices

There are 24 indices, which hold integer values only. The appropriate programming manual should be consulted for the range of values that an index can hold on a particular computer. The indices use letters in the ranges

$$I-T \qquad I'-T'$$

The index T$'$ has a special use, and since its value can be changed by certain statements in the course of the program its use is best avoided.

Main variables

Most programs will need more store than can be provided by the 24 indices and 30 special variables. The main variables consist of a letter in the range

$$A-H \qquad U-\pi$$

followed by a suffix or subscript. Acceptable main variables would be

$$E45 \quad \pi6 \quad U0 \quad B500$$

There is no connection between a letter used as a special variable and the same letter used with a suffix as a main variable. The value stored in special variable F, for instance, has no connection whatever with any of the values stored in the main variables F0, F1, etc.

Special variables and indices can be used in any EMA program without being specially requested by the programmer. Main variables have to be requested since the quantity a program uses is not fixed. If he wished to use 500 main variables, the programmer would write at the head of a program

MAIN 500

The programmer would also write the letters it was desired to use with the highest suffix required with each letter in the following form:

$$A \rightarrow 399$$
$$X \rightarrow 29$$
$$D \rightarrow 49$$

Main variables are a one-dimensional array having a lower bound of zero so that, in the above example, 400 As, 30 Xs and 50 Ds have been requested. It is common to request a few more variables with the MAIN directive than are actually used to allow for subsequent program alterations.

The suffix of a main variable need not be an integer. Other forms that it can take include an index and an arithmetic expression combining indices and integers. If J had the value 4 and K had the value 7,

AK would be equivalent to A7
A(K+J) would be equivalent to A11
A(K−J+2) would be equivalent to A5.

The utility of being able to use suffices of the above form will be seen later.

Constants

We often need to refer to a numerical value directly in a program. If so, we can use a constant. A constant can be written, signed or unsigned, in conventional decimal notation. The following are examples of EMA constants:

$$+3.19 \quad -78.906 \quad 0.87 \quad .765 \quad -017 \quad 00.0019200 \quad \& \quad 8$$

To avoid writing strings of zeros, the form using & can be used. & followed by an integer (signed or unsigned) means that the number before & is multiplied by the power of ten represented by the integer.

1.9&2 represents $1.9 \times 10^2 = 190$
37&−2 represents $37 \times 10^{-2} = .37$
&4 represents $10^4 = 10,000$

The number after & must not contain & or a decimal point.

Arithmetic expressions

The form of an EMA arithmetic instruction is

variable = arithmetic expression

The simplest form of an arithmetic expression is a variable or constant, so that simple arithmetic expressions could be

A = B
K = 7

If a real arithmetic expression is stored in an index the value is rounded to the nearest integer so that

I = 4.3 would store 4 in I
I = 4.8 would store 5 in I

Variables and constants can be combined by arithmetic operators to form arithmetic expressions. The arithmetic operators are:

$$+ \qquad * \text{ (multiply)}$$
$$- \qquad / \text{ (divide)}$$

Parentheses can be nested to any depth and redundant parentheses are ignored by the compiler. Both round parentheses and square brackets can be used in pairs. Both types can be used in the same arithmetic expression. The operator * can be omitted except in two cases:

1. The product of two constants. It is obvious that (3.176 * 789) cannot be written as (3.176789.)
2. The product of an unprimed special variable and a quantity with the same form as a main variable suffix if the variable comes first.

A1 refers to an item in the set of main variables A.
IA refers to the product of special variable A and I.
W7 refers to an item in the set of main variables W.
7W refers to the product of 7 and the special variable W.
E(I+J) refers to an item on the set of main variables E.
(I+J)E refers to the product of special variable E and (I+J).

To avoid ambiguity the beginner is recommended to use asterisks for multiplication.

The divisor after / must be a constant, single variable, function or bracketed arithmetic expression.

An arithmetic expression is evaluated from left to right with * and / taking precedence over + and −, unless overridden by parentheses. Thus

$$G+H-W+X*D \quad \text{is equivalent to} \quad G+H-W+(X*D).$$

A suffix must be an integer expression, which can only contain an integer constant and an index (and an integer function, which is defined in the next section. The divide operator, /, is *not* allowed in an integer expression.

The expressions A8, H(T+5), use acceptable suffices.

The expressions A8.0, H(T/5), do not use acceptable suffices.

Functions

Brief reference has already been made to functions in the previous section. The power of an arithmetic expression can be enhanced by the inclusion of the functions listed below, which save the programmer much effort.

All functions are preceded by the Greek letter ϕ, and the argument of the function, which can be an arithmetic expression and can itself contain a function, is enclosed in parentheses.

In the list below, which contains the most common functions, X and Y represent arithmetic expressions and M and N integer expressions.

General functions

ϕ SQRT(X)		$X \geqslant 0$
ϕ EXP(X)	e^X	
ϕ LOG(X)	$\log_e X$	$X > 0$
ϕ MOD(X)	absolute value of X $\quad \lvert X \rvert$	
ϕ FRPT(X)	fractional part of X	
	$(X - \phi\text{INTPT(X)})$ see below)	
ϕ SIN(X)	sin x	x in radians
ϕ COS(X)	cos x	x in radians
ϕ TAN(X)	tan x	x in radians
ϕ ARCSIN(X)	$-\dfrac{\pi}{2} \leqslant \sin^{-1} X \leqslant \dfrac{\pi}{2}$	$-1 \leqslant X \leqslant 1$
ϕ ARCCOS(X)	$0 \leqslant \cos^{-1} X \leqslant \pi$	$-1 \leqslant X \leqslant 1$
ϕ ARCTAN(X)	$-\dfrac{\pi}{2} < \tan^{-1} X < \dfrac{\pi}{2}$	
ϕ ARCTAN(X, Y)	$-\pi < \tan^{-1}(Y/X) \leqslant \pi$	$X^2 + Y^2 \neq 0$

the quadrant is determined as if X and Y are proportional to the cosine and sine of the angle respectively.

ϕ RADIUS(X, Y) $\quad \sqrt{(X^2 + Y^2)}$

Integer functions

ϕ INTPT(X) the largest integer $\leqslant (X)$

ϕ SIGN(X) 1 if $X \geqslant 0$; -1 if $X < 0$

ϕ PARITY(M) 1 if M even; -1 if M odd

ϕ MAX(A0, M, N)
ϕ MIN(A0, M, N)

the suffix of the largest (or smallest) element of the set AM, A(M+1), ..., AN. If there is no unique largest or smallest element, the one with the maximum (or minimum) value and lowest suffix is taken.

The integer functions can have only integer values and can be used as suffixes, for example,

HϕINTPT(B−D)
E(6+ϕPARITY(L'))

Exponentiation of positive quantities can be obtained by using ϕLOG and ϕEXP in conjunction, for example,

ϕEXP(4.6 * ϕLOG(X)) gives $X^{4.6}$
ϕEXP(ϕLOG(X)/3) gives $\sqrt[3]{(X)}$

The definition of ϕINTPT implies that ϕINTPT(-3.1) and ϕINTPT(-3.99) both have the value of -4.

Sometimes there is confusion about the purpose of ϕMAX and ϕMIN, which give the *suffix* of the largest (or smallest) element in a set. If the values of the elements G1 — G4 were 8, 19, 1 and -3, the instruction

$$K = \phi MAX(G0, 1, 4)$$

would put the value 2 in K since G2 contains the largest value. If it was desired to store the largest element of the array G in Y, the integer function ϕMAX could be used as a suffix

$$Y = G\phi MAX(G0, 1, 4)$$

Input

The form of the READ instruction is

READ(variable or index)

For instance, it might be

READ(J)
READ(D)

This takes the next number from the data document and stores it in the variable or index.

The numbers can be punched in any of the forms allowable as program constants (see the section on *Constants*). Each number must be terminated by a newline character, by at least two spaces, or by a prime ($'$). Extra spaces and newlines are ignored. Single spaces are allowed in a number. More than one space terminates a number except after an ampersand.

156& -4

is acceptable

—   876

is faulty.

In a data document (*not* in a program) an ampersand can be replaced by a comma so the above number could be also punched as

156, -4

If any character other than a digit, terminator, sign, &, comma or space is read by this instruction, a read error occurs.

If a real number is read into an index, only the integral part is stored. If the item of data was -7.01, the instruction

READ(K)

would store -8 in K.

Printing

The basic print instruction is

PRINT(X)m, n

where X is an arithmetic expression, m is the number of places before the point and n is the number of places after the point. These are sometimes referred to as format positions. Insignificant zeros are suppressed so that if X contained 17.6 the instruction

PRINT(X)3, 2

would print

17.60

— is printed if the number is negative. A number is automatically followed by two spaces, which cannot be suppressed. If a number is positive, a space is printed instead of a minus sign.

If it is desired to print an integer value, 0 is put after the comma in the format, for example,

PRINT(K)6, 0

Whatever style of printing is used the number is correctly rounded. If X had the value 6.76:

PRINT(X)1, 1

would print 6.8;

PRINT(X)1, 0

would print 7.

0 in the first format position is best not used by a beginner. Since a number is always preceded by a minus sign or space and followed by two spaces the style

PRINT(X)m, n

uses $m+n+4$ print positions;

PRINT(X)m, 0

uses $m+3$ print positions.

NEWLINE

results in the next command for the printer starting on the next line.

NEWLINE2

moves to the next line but one and leaves one blank line.

NEWLINE(m)

leaves m − 1 blank lines.
The following section of program

    PRINT(A)3, 2
    NEWLINE
    PRINT(B)3, 2
    NEWLINE
    PRINT(D)3, 2

could print

    123.45
    −9.00
    12345.67

It will be observed that enough integer places are not specified for the third number, and that the decimal point is moved to the right. If such a quantity was in error it could therefore be easily detected. Sometimes the instruction

    PRINT(X)1, 1

is used to obtain left justification of printed quantities. It is important to emphasize that there is no loss of significant digits.

Text can be printed by enclosing the desired symbols between primes so that the instruction

    PRINT('SATURDAY')

would print

    SATURDAY

Spaces are significant inside the primes. The instruction

    PRINT('8 MARCH 1969')

contains a space after 8 and after MARCH and would print

    8 MARCH 1969

No extra spaces are inserted by this instruction, so if X had the value of −3.25 the following sequence of instructions

    PRINT('X=')
    PRINT(X)1, 2

would print

    X = −3.25

The first PRINT instruction for a line printer in a program commences printing in the first character position of the first line of a new page. Two instructions in addition to NEWLINE are provided to assist in obtaining a desired layout on a printed page.

SPACE(n)

where n is an integer expression gives extra spaces. If only a single space is required, SPACE is equivalent to SPACE1. An unsigned integer need not be put in brackets, for example,

SPACE 6.

An expression must be bracketed, for example,

SPACE(K + M)

The instruction

RUNOUT

causes the line printer to throw to the head of the next page. The name is derived from its action with a paper tape punch, which it causes to output about six inches of runout.

Transfer of control

An EMA program is obeyed instruction by instruction in the written order. Sometimes we need to depart from this strict sequence. If we wish to resume sequential working at a certain instruction, that instruction must have a *label*. A label is written before the instruction to which it refers, and is separated from it by a round bracket. It consists of an unsigned integer between 0 and 127 (0 and 100 are used for special purposes and should be avoided normally). A typical labelled instruction could be

7)A = B + C

Labels can be used in any order. An instruction can have any number of labels, for example,

9)17)92) I = 8

but this is seldom (if ever) necessary.

The simplest form of transfer instruction is JUMP. The instruction

JUMP 89

would jump to the instruction with label 89 and obey instructions sequentially from that point.

One of the most powerful and useful features of a digital computer is the facility of choosing between various courses of action depending on whether or not a given condition is true. This facility is provided in EMA by the conditional JUMP instruction, which has the general form

JUMP   *label, arithmetic expression relational operator arithmetic expression*

The relational operators are

$$= \qquad \geqslant$$
$$\neq \qquad <$$
$$> \qquad \leqslant$$

Typical conditional jump instructions could be

JUMP 7, K = 5
JUMP 95, ϕSQRT(U + V) > E * G

If the condition is true, a jump is made to the labelled instruction and instructions are obeyed sequentially from that point. If the condition is not true, the next instruction is obeyed.

In the following (trivial) sequence of instructions:

K = 9
L = 8
JUMP 6, K + L = 17
PRINT(L)2, 0
6) ...

control would go to the instruction with label 6, and the print instruction would not be obeyed.

= and $\neq$ should only be used to compare integer expressions, since expressions in floating-point representation may not be evaluated exactly and will be equal only by chance.

Instead of writing

JUMP 5, X − Y = G + H

one should write

JUMP 5, ϕMOD((X − Y) + (G − H)) < & − 10

Any minute quantity could be substituted for & − 10.

A complete program

In order that the examples in the next section can have realistic solutions it is necessary to show how the instructions so far encountered can be incorporated in a complete program. The following short program prints the squares and cubes of numbers from one to ten.

```
      MAIN 0
      CHAPTER 0
      N = 1      |starting value
  1)  M = N * N
      L = M * N
      PRINT(N)3, 0
      PRINT(M)6, 0
      PRINT(L)9, 0
      NEWLINE
      N = N + 1
      JUMP 1, N < 11
      END
      CLOSE
```

Comment is preceded by a vertical bar and is used above after the instruction $N = 1$.

Chapters are discussed in a later section. Small programs can be written conveniently under the heading CHAPTER 0.

CLOSE signifies the end of the *text* of a chapter and is a directive to indicate to the compiler that anything following CLOSE is not part of that chapter.

END is used when we wish to stop obeying program instructions, and it is equivalent to an instruction to terminate the execution of the program. A program can have many END instructions. The following sequence of instructions reads ten numbers and prints out the square root, but if the number read is $\leqslant 0$ it prints out NO ROOT and then stops.

```
      I = 1
  3)  READ(X)
      JUMP 1, X > 0
      PRINT('NO ROOT')
      END
  1)  PRINT(φSQRT(X))4, 4
      I = I + 1
      JUMP 3, I < 11
      END
```

Exercises 8.1†

1. Print the integers 1–100 followed by their squares, cubes, square roots and cube roots.

† Suggested solutions to all exercises follow after chapter 8.

2. Read in 12 sales amounts for the 12 months, and print each as a ratio to January, with January = 100.

3. Read ten numbers, compute and print the average, and print the number with the greatest absolute deviation from the average.

4. Write a sequence of instructions to print out the largest element of a matrix with three rows and four columns; also to print out the row and column of the largest element.

5. $\pi/4 = 1 - \frac{1}{3} + \frac{1}{5} - \frac{1}{7} + \frac{1}{9}$ ....
   Evaluate 1000 terms of this series and print out the value of π to eight decimal places every 100 terms.

6. Print the prime numbers between three and 100.

7. Compute and print the terms of the Fibonacci series

   $$X_{n+1} = X_n + X_{n-1}$$

   between 10^5 and 10^8. The first few terms are

   0 1 1 2 3 5 8 ....

8. The solution of the simultaneous equations

   $$ax + by + c = 0$$
   $$px + qy + r = 0$$

   is given by

   $$x = (br - cq)/(aq - bp)$$
   $$y = (pc - ar)/aq - bp)$$

   Read a, b, c, p, q, r and compute and print x and y.
   Print INDETERMINATE if $aq - bp = 0$
   Print NOT INDEPENDENT if $a/p = b/q = c/r$.

Simple loops

A more concise way of writing the example in the previous section for printing out squares and cubes of numbers between one and ten would be:

```
MAIN 0
CHAPTER 0
N = 1(1)10
M = N * N
L = N * M
PRINT(N)3, 0
PRINT(M)6, 0
PRINT(L)9, 0
NEWLINE
REPEAT
END
CLOSE
```

The simple loop in the above example was defined by the pair of instructions

N = 1(1)10

and

REPEAT

The *body* of the loop is the instructions between these two. The body is executed with N taking the initial value of 1, and then is repeated with N being increased by 1 until the last time through the loop when the body is repeated with N taking the value of 10.

The general form of the first loop instruction is

I = J(K)L

or

I = J(−K)L

The body of the loop is repeatedly obeyed with I taking the values

J, J+K, J+2K, ..., L.

I is known as the controlled index.

Only the increment can have a negative sign. J and L can be replaced by an unsigned integer, and K can be replaced by an integer or integer with a negative sign. If we wish to have a loop with the initial and terminal values negative, these values must be stored in indices so that negative signs are not written in the loop initialization instruction, for example,

```
K = −1
L = −10
T = K(−1)L
... ...
... ...
REPEAT
```

Only one REPEAT is allowed for each simple loop. If at any point in the body of the loop we wish to repeat the loop, we must do this by a JUMP to REPEAT, for example,

```
     N = 1(1)100
     READ(AN)
     JUMP 45, AN < 0
     T = T+AN
45)  REPEAT
```

The difference between the initial and terminal value should be a positive multiple of the increment, otherwise the loop can cycle indefinitely as in the following example.

T = 9
R = 4(2)T
... ...
REPEAT

Here R would take the value 4, 6, 8, 10, 12, 14, ...
In the loop

K = 1
I = 1(4)K
... ...
REPEAT

the loop would be obeyed once only with I taking the value 1.

The value of the controlled index and terminal and initial values should not be changed in the body of the loop. The controlled index should not also appear as the initial or terminal value.

There should be no jump into the body of the loop (thus bypassing the setting of the controlled index) unless there has been a jump out of it.

The following structure is allowed.

19) I = J(K)L
     ... ...
     JUMP 8
17) ... ...
     REPEAT
     ... ...
8)   ... ...
     ... ...
     JUMP 17

whereas the following is faulty:

     I = J(K)L
     ... ...
98) ... ...
     REPEAT
     ... ...
     JUMP 98

Loops within loops are allowed, but there must be no more than 24 loop instructions awaiting their repeat. Loops and repeats are matched like left and right parentheses so there is no confusion as to which repeat belongs to which loop instruction.

In the following example it is desired to use the formula $X = I/J$ to tabulate X for combinations of I and J, with I taking the values from 100 to 500 in steps of 10 and J taking the values from 1 to 10 in steps of 1:

```
I = 100(10)500
J = 1(1)10
X = I/J
PRINT(X)3, 0
NEWLINE
REPEAT
REPEAT
```

Exercises 8.2

Do questions 1-6 of Exercises 8.1 using simple loops.

Subroutines

We often need to use common sequence of instructions at different points in the program. The idea was demonstrated in chapter 2, where it was referred to as a subroutine.

The simplest and most usual manner of writing a subroutine in EMA is to write it as a normal sequence of instructions with a RETURN instruction at each point where it is desired to return to the main sequence. The subroutine is then entered by a JUMPDOWN instruction to the appropriate label.

The following program reads ten quantities of millimetres, prints each as metres and centimetres, and prints their average in the same manner.

```
       MAIN 0
       CHAPTER 0
       J = 0
       N = 1(1)10
       READ(K)
       J = J + K
       JUMPDOWN 1
       REPEAT
       K = φINTPT(J/10)
       JUMPDOWN 1
       END
   1)  L = φINTPT(K/1000)
       PRINT(L) 3, 0
       R = K - 1000L
       JUMP 2, R = 0
       S = φINTPT(R/10)
       P = R - 10S
```

3)   PRINT(S) 2, 0
      PRINT(P) 2, 0
      NEWLINE
      RETURN
2)   S = 0
      P = 0
      JUMP 3
      CLOSE

The subroutine is entered twice in the program and on each occasion returns to the instruction after the appropriate JUMPDOWN. It will be observed that the subroutine expects to find a quantity of millimetres in K and returns values to the main program in L, S and P and assumes that K will not contain a value of 0. Often a subroutine can be written generally by one programmer and used by several others. In that case the importance of full and adequate documentation of the subroutine with regard to indices and variables used cannot be too strongly emphasized. The above subroutine uses R as working storage and does not alter the value of K. It is not usual for a subroutine to alter the value of the variable or index which contains the argument on which the subroutine is to work.

A subroutine can call another by means of a JUMPDOWN instruction.

Chapters

The previous sections have described the basic features of the language, and most programs of a numerical nature can be written in this basic subset of the language. The rest of this section will deal with some of the facilities and refinements that can often with great advantage be incorporated into an EMA program.

All EMA programs so far encountered have been written in a single chapter, Chapter 0. A program can be broken down into several chapters; indeed on the original Mercury computer this was essential because of store limitations. A program of great length can be written in a single chapter for Atlas, Orion or the 1900 series computers, but often it is considered advantageous to break down a long program into chapters of about 100 instructions. Each chapter would contain a well-defined section of the whole program.

A chapter has the heading

CHAPTER n

where n is an integer between 0 and 4095, and the end of the text of a chapter is marked by the word

CLOSE

Chapter 0 must be written last, yet the first instruction to be obeyed in the program is the first instruction in Chapter 0. Apart from that, chapter numbers can be used in any order: a program could have a weird numbering scheme of Chapters 56, 192, 60, 0! Each chapter has its own set of labels from 0 to 127 so that if a programmer exhausts all the label numbers in a single chapter he will be compelled to have another chapter.

A program does not flow automatically from the end of one chapter to the beginning of the next. Communication between chapters is effected by the ACROSS instruction, which has the general form

ACROSS label/ chapter

An example could be

ACROSS 6/191

which would jump to label 6 of Chapter 191 and commence obeying instructions sequentially from that point. A JUMP instruction only refers to a label in the same chapter. There is no conditional form of the ACROSS instruction.

Special variables and indices are common to all chapters, and the only value that is altered by an ACROSS instruction is π, which is reset to 3.1415926536.

Main variables are local to a chapter. If the same main variables are required in more than one chapter they must be re-declared, for example,

MAIN 300
CHAPTER 1
X → 99
Y → 149
CLOSE
CHAPTER 0
X → 99
Y → 149
CLOSE

In the above example both chapters use the same main variables. This could have been indicated by writing the directive

VARIABLES 1

at the head of Chapter 0. A VARIABLES directive can be used with any chapter number except 0. The directive VARIABLES 1 at the head of a chapter indicates that the variables declared in Chapter 1 apply to the following chapter. A VARIABLES directive can refer to any chapter previously written. It can be followed by the declaration of further main variables local to a particular chapter.

In the following example:

```
MAIN 320
CHAPTER 5
A → 99
B → 49
CLOSE
CHAPTER 7
VARIABLES 5
D → 49
E → 49
CLOSE
CHAPTER 0
VARIABLES 7
F → 49
CLOSE
```

Chapter 5 can use main variables A and B, Chapter 7 can use main variables A, B, D, E and F. A considerable amount of ingenuity can be used in the manipulation of main variables in a program with more than one chapter. The reader is referred to the appropriate programming manual for details.

The MAIN directive is common to all chapters and may not be repeated.

A subroutine entered by a JUMPDOWN cannot be referred to outside the chapter in which it is written, since labels are local to a particular chapter. If it is desired to have a subroutine common to several chapters, that subroutine is entered by the DOWN instruction that has the general form

DOWN label/chapter

For example,

DOWN 78/157

would enter a subroutine at label 78 of Chapter 157.

A subroutine used in more than one chapter has UP whenever it is desired to return control to the original chapter at the instruction after DOWN. This type of subroutine can extend to more than one chapter.

The example from the previous section is rewritten below with the subroutine in Chapter 7:

```
       MAIN 0
       CHAPTER 7
1)     L − φINTPT(K/1000)
       PRINT(L)3, 0
       R = K − 1000L
       JUMP 2, R = 0
       S = φINTPT(R/10)
       P = R − 10S
```

3) PRINT(S) 2, 0
    PRINT(P) 2, 0
    NEWLINE
    UP
2) S = 0
    P = 0
    JUMP 3
    CLOSE
    CHAPTER 0
    J = 0
    N = 1(1)10
    READ(K)
    J = J + K
    DOWN 1/7
    REPEAT
    K − φINTPT(J/10)
    DOWN 1/7
    END
    CLOSE

Communication between sections in different chapters is effected by the
ACROSS instruction. The UP can therefore be in a different chapter to
the beginning of the subroutine.

Further subroutine facilities

A subroutine can be written as a self-contained ROUTINE available to
all chapters in the program. A ROUTINE is headed by

ROUTINE n

where n is an integer between 0 and 4095, and the end of the text is marked
by two asterisks on a new line.

**

Entry is by an instruction of the form

JUMPDOWN(Rn)

where n is the number of the ROUTINE, or of the form

JUMPDOWN(Rn/label)

where n is the ROUTINE number and label refers to the label number of a
particular ROUTINE. (Labels are local to a particular ROUTINE;
labels 0 and 100 have no special significance.)

Exit from a ROUTINE is effected by a RETURN instruction.

A ROUTINE may have a JUMPDOWN to another ROUTINE.

A ROUTINE cannot be written inside a chapter or another ROUTINE. It must be written before the chapters that use it. It is customary to write all the ROUTINES used in a program after the MAIN directive and before any chapters. The values of variables and indices are unchanged on entry to a ROUTINE. The compiler inserts a copy of the ROUTINE in any chapter that uses it, and the ROUTINE usually refers to the main variables in the containing chapter. A ROUTINE can contain its own main variables; these follow on from the end of these in the containing chapter as the following example demonstrates.

```
MAIN 320
ROUTINE 31
X→4
Y→14
**
ROUTINE 38
Z→19
**
ROUTINE 22
**
CHAPTER 1
A→49
B →49
JUMPDOWN(R31)
JUMPDOWN(R38)
CLOSE
CHAPTER 0
VARIABLES 1
D→49
JUMPDOWN(R38)
JUMPDOWN(R22)
CLOSE
```

The main variables available in different parts of this program are:

Chapter 1	A0–49, B0–49
Routine 31 in Chapter 1	A0–49, B0–49, X0–4, Y0–14
Routine 38 in Chapter 1	A0–49, B0–49, Z0–19
Chapter 0	A0–49, B0–49, D0–49
Routine 38 in Chapter 0	A0–49, B0–49, D0–49, Z0–19
Routine 22 in Chapter 0	As Chapter 0

VARIABLES directives are not allowed inside a ROUTINE.

Large subroutines can be written in several of their own chapters as PROGRAMMES. This technique will rarely be needed by a beginner, and details will be given in the appropriate programming manual.

Character manipulation

If we wish to read a single character, the appropriate instruction is

READCH(index)

The index will contain the character code for the character. If we wish to print the single character contained in an index, the instruction has the form

PRINTCH(index)

This prints a single character only.

If a tape contains the characters SG*, the instructions

READCH(L)
READCH(M)
READCH(N)

will store S in L, G in M and * in N, respectively. The instructions

PRINTCH(N)
PRINTCH(M)
PRINTCH(L)

would print

* GS

In character manipulation it is essential to be able to recognize a character read. This is achieved in EMA by the integer function ϕCODE. ϕCODE(&) provides the code of the character &, whilst the instruction

T = ϕCODE(Y)

sets T to this value. A subsequent instruction

PRINTCH(T)

would print

Y

The following sequence of instructions reads and prints characters until a full stop is encountered:

```
2)  READCH(T)
    JUMP 1, T ≠ φCODE(.)
    END
1)  PRINTCH(T)
    JUMP 2
```

The programmer need not be concerned about the integer value of the character-code, which varies with the computer used. Some characters have to be represented by abbreviations. ϕCODE(SP) and ϕCODE(NL) represent a single space and newline character.

These characters are *not* skipped by the READCH instruction as they are if they appear in a number read by the READ instruction.

The characters

    SH E
    ENA

read by the sequence of instructions

    READCH(I)
    READCH(J)
    READCH(K)
    READCH(L)
    READCH(M)
    READCH(N)
    READCH(O)
    READCH(P)

would put the following values in the indices:

    I ϕCODE(S)
    J ϕCODE(H)
    K ϕCODE(SP)
    L ϕCODE(E)
    M ϕCODE(NL)
    N ϕCODE(E)
    O ϕCODE(N)
    P ϕCODE(A)

It will be seen that space and newline are both stored. Some characters such as 'erase' and the shifts on paper tape are removed from the tape before it is read. Reference should be made to the appropriate programming manual for details of these and for details of paper-tape control characters such as 'tab' (a character that causes a jump to the next tabulating position), since treatment of these varies from one computer to another.

Although it is not necessary to know the numerical values of the character codes, certain relationships can be assumed. ϕCODE(Z) is equal to ϕCODE(A)$+25$, ϕCODE(9) is equal to ϕCODE(0)$+9$ and ϕCODE(SP)$<\phi$CODE(A). This information can be useful in simple sorting.

Since there are only 24 indices, variables can be used to hold characters if it is essential to hold a large number of them.

A main or special variable can be regarded as having four positions in which characters can be inserted or 'packed'. These positions are numbered 0–3. The general form of the PACK instruction is

PACK(*variable, packing position, index*).

The character held in the index S would be put into packing position 1 of H31 by the instruction

PACK(H31, 1, S).

A PACK instruction does not affect any other character position except the one referenced in the instruction. In the above example, the contents of packing positions 0, 2 and 3 of H31 are undisturbed.

The main variables can be regarded as a continuous string of packing positions so that position 2 of A1 is the same as position 6 of A0. The following example will clarify this.

Variable	Position			
	0	1	2	3
A0	N	I	C	H
A1	O	L	A	S
A2	,	F	I	O
A3	N	A	.	

The start of FIONA could be referred to by a PACK instruction as PACK(A2, 1, K) or PACK(A0, 9, K) or PACK(A1, 5, K). Negative position numbers are not allowed.

If we wish to take characters out of the packing positions, the UNPACK instruction, of the same general form as the PACK instruction is used. The instruction

UNPACK(H4, 3, S)

would put the character in packing position 3 of H4 into the index S.

The following sequence of instructions prints 300 characters stored in the main variables G0–G74. It is assumed that the characters include the appropriate newline characters.

N = 0(1)299
UNPACK(G0, N, J)
PRINTCH(J)
REPEAT

This is an appropriate point to discuss the use of label 0 in a chapter. If an illegal character (see the section on *Input*) is read by a READ instruction, the program automatically jumps to label 0 in the chapter.

If there is not a label 0, the fault is monitored in the usual way. A sequence of instructions can be written that commence at label 0 to rectify the situation. The first instruction of the sequence should be a READCH instruction to obtain the spurious character. This facility is often employed to identify an alphabetic character used to terminate a series of numbers of unknown length. The following small program reads numbers from paper tape until the character Z is encountered, and then prints the average of the numbers and the number of items read. It will be noticed that if any illegal character other than Z is encountered the program ignores the rest of the line.

```
        MAIN 0
        CHAPTER 0
        Y = 0
        N = 0
   1)   READ(X)
        Y = Y + X
        N = N + 1
        JUMP 1
   0)   READCH(M)                        | reads faulty character
        JUMP 2, M = φCODE(Z)
        JUMP 0, M ≠ φCODE(NL)            | reads until newline found
        JUMP 1                           | returns when newline found
   2)   A = Y/N
        PRINT('AVERAGE = ')
        PRINT(A)3, 3
        NEWLINE
        PRINT('NUMBER OF ITEMS')
        PRINT(N)3, 0
        END
        CLOSE
```

Tables

Tables can be written as part of the program instead of being read in as data. A chapter can have a table of general constants of a form such as

```
   31)    192.3
          + 22.3
   12)    1.23&5
          43.576
          − 11.85
```

The first line of such a table must be labelled. Labels on other lines are optional.

The ϕTABLE instruction, of the general form

ϕTABLE(*label*, position)

can be used to reference an item in a table. The instruction

Y = ϕTABLE(31, 3)

would put the value of 43.576 in Y. The first position of the table is position 0. The instruction

Y = ϕTABLE(12, 1)

would put the same value in Y.

The instruction naturally must be in the same chapter as the table.

There can be any number of tables in a chapter. The programmer must ensure that no attempt is made to obey a table entry as an instruction; the instruction before a table should be an unconditional jump, END or ACROSS.

Integer constants can be stored more compactly by an integer constants table. Each line of such a table begins with the word INTEGERS and should contain an even number of entries (a zero entry is added automatically to any line containing an odd number of entries). Entries are separated from each other by commas. A typical integer table could be:

21)   INTEGERS 9, −1, +57, 8
      INTEGERS 98, −56, 192, 154, 403

It must be remembered that ϕCODE is an integer function and therefore can be used in an integer constants table. There is no limit to the number of lines in a table.

ϕTABLE cannot appear in an arithmetic expression. Only a special or main variable can appear on the left-hand side of an instruction referencing a general constants table and only an index on the left-hand side of an integer constants table.

The following trivial sequence of instructions reads a code number of 50 items from paper tape and prints the balances in hand from a table arranged in code number order:

        N = 1(1)50
        READ(J)
        K = ϕTABLE(1, J−1)
        PRINT(J)3, 0
        PRINT(K)4, 0
        NEWLINE
        REPEAT
        END

1) INTEGERS 8765,4321,765,45

... ...

INTEGERS 7643,23,48,85
CLOSE

Magnetic tape instructions

Magnetic tape and its uses were described in chapter 1. Data in EMA are transferred to and from magnetic tape in numbered *blocks* that can hold 512 variables. Block 0 is not for programmer use. A particular computer installation will supply details of the number of blocks on individual magnetic tapes. An individual tape is given a number in the range 0–7. A tape is wound to the start of a desired block by the WIND TAPE instruction.

WIND TAPE(0, 192)

would wind tape 0 backwards or forwards to the start of block 192. If it were desired to copy the values of variables H0–511 to that block, the appropriate instruction would be

WRITE(0, H0).

This would copy the values of the variables to block 192 and leave H0–511 undisturbed. The tape would now be moved into a position ready for data to be transferred to or from block 193. It should never be assumed at the start of a program that a tape is positioned to the start of block 1.

The most common read instruction is READ FWD. The instruction

READ FWD(2, G101)

would read the next block on the tape to main variables G101–612 and move the tape to the start of the next block.

On some tape systems tape can be read when moving backwards. The instruction

READ BKD(2, H101)

given immediately after the READFWD instruction above would read the same block as was read to G101–612 to H101–612. If these data were on block 80, the tape would now be moved into a position to work forwards on block 80 or backwards on block 79. The only difference between the two read instructions is that the tape is left in a different position. The first variable in the block is always transferred to the main variable mentioned in the instruction. Data are not reversed in any way! Tape should be read backwards whenever this minimizes the amount of tape winding.

A tape is rewound to block 1 if the tape number is specified in a REWIND instruction such as

REWIND(5)

which rewinds tape 5 to the start of block 1.

When a particular tape is no longer needed by a program it can be relinquished by an instruction such as

RELINQUISH DECK(3).

After this instruction tape 3 could not be referred to again by the program. A REWIND instruction is not essential before a tape is relinquished.

If a 1900 series computer is being used when a block is written, any blocks of higher number will be lost so that a WRITE instruction cannot be followed by a READ or WIND TAPE instruction referring to a higher-numbered block.

The following sequence of instructions reads numbers from paper tape until an asterisk is found, writes them to tape and fills up the unused portion of the last block with zeros.

	WIND TAPE(0, 1)	| tape at start of block 1
1)	N = 0	
2)	READ(YN)	
	N = N + 1	
	JUMP 2, N < 512	
	WRITE(0, Y0)	
	JUMP 1	
0)	READCH(M)	| non-numeric character read (see under *Character Manipulation*
	JUMP 3, M = ϕCODE(*)	| end of data read
	JUMP 0, M ≠ ϕCODE(NL)	| reads until newline found-faulty data
	JUMP 2	| returns when newline found
3)	I = N(1)511	
	YI = 0	
	REPEAT	| unused portion zero-filled
	WRITE(0, Y0)	| writes last block

The basic features of EMA have now been discussed. There are some specialized features that will generate pseudo-random numbers, perform matrix operations and perform bit manipulation. There are also important diagnostic aids, which vary from one computer to another. The appropriate programming manual should be consulted for these features.

Exercises 8.3

1. Read a series of numbers ending with an asterisk and print the average, largest and smallest of the numbers. Assume there are no more than 1000 numbers.
2. A paper tape contains not more than 100 numbers ending with an asterisk, and it is known that it contains some erroneous characters. Print out the number of erroneous characters and the number of negative numbers on the tape.
3. Read a series of ten numbers. Print the square and reciprocal of each and the square and reciprocal of their average.
4. A sentence of not more than 500 characters contains only one full stop at the end and has at least one space after each word. Read in the sentence and print out the number of words.
5. Read a series of numbers ending with an asterisk to magnetic tape from paper tape. Print out the block and word (in the range 1–512) containing the last number, and print out the largest number. It can be assumed that all numbers are positive, that the first block written is block 1 and that the number of items is not an exact multiple of 512.

SUGGESTED SOLUTIONS

It was mentioned in chapter 2 that there are often many different, but equally correct, solutions to a programming problem. When the variety of different identifiers that can be used in high-level programming languages is recalled, it will be evident that there is almost an infinity of possible solutions. Therefore the following are suggestions for correct solutions. In most cases identifiers have been kept short and the use of ingenious short cuts avoided.

Exercises 4.1

1.
```
begin integer; n, square;
     n:=1;
start: square:=n * n; print(n, 3, 0); print(square, 6, 0);
       print(n * square, 9, 0); print(sqrt(n), 2, 4);
       print(n ↑ (1/3), 2, 4); newline(1); n:=n+1;
       if n < 101 then goto start
end
```

2.
```
begin integer n; real recip;
     n:=2;
start: recip:=1/n; print(recip, 1, 6); newline(1); n:=n+1;
       if n < 101 then goto start
end
```

3.
```
begin integer jan, sales, count;
     real ratio; jan:=read; count:=0; sales:=jan;
     L1: ratio:=(sales/jan) * 100;
     print(ratio, 3, 3); newline(1);
     count:=count+1; if count < 12
     then begin sales:=read; goto L1;
     end
end
```

4.
```
begin integer count; real x, y, h;
     count:=0;
L1: x:=read; y:=read; h = sqrt(x ↑ 2+y ↑ 2); print(h, 3, 3);
    newline(1); count:=count+1;
    if count < 10 then goto L1;
end
```

167

5.

```
begin integer a; real r;
    a:=1;
start: r:=sqrt(a/3.14); print(a, 3, 0); print(r, 3, 2); newline(1);
    a:=a+1; if a<101 then goto start
end
```

6.

```
begin integer count1, n, count2, n; real p, term;
    p:=0; count1:=count2:=0; n:=1; term:=1;
start: term:=sign(term) * (1/n); p:=p+term; n: = n+2;
    term:= -term; count2:=count2+1; if count2<100 then
    goto start; count2:=0; print(4 * p, 1, 8); newline(1);
    count1:=count1+1; if count1<10 then goto start
end
```

7.

```
begin integer n1, n2, n3;
    n1:=0; n2:=1;
start: n3:=n2+n1; n1:=n2; n2:=n3; if n3<10 ↑ 5 then goto
    start; if n3<10 ↑ 8 then
                    begin print(n3, 10, 0); newline(1);
                    goto start;
                    end
end
```

8.

```
begin real a, b, c, d, e, p, q, r, x, y;
    a:=read; b:=read; c:=read; p:=read; q:=read; r:=read;
    d:=a * q-b * p; s:=b * r-c * q; if abs(d)<₁₀-10 then
        begin if abs(e)<₁₀-10 then
            begin writetext(({NOT})); space(2);
            writetext(({INDEPENDENT})); goto finish
            end;
        writetext(({INDETERMINATE})); goto finish
        end;
    x:=e/d; y:=(p * c-a * r)/d; print(x, 3, 3); print(y, 3, 3);
finish: end
```

Exercises 4.2

1.
```
begin integer n, square;
    for n:=1 step 1 until 100 do
        begin square:=n * n; print(n, 3, 0); print(square, 6, 0);
        print(n * square, 9, 0); print(sqrt(n), 2, 4);
        print(n ↑ (1/3), 2, 4); newline(1)
        end
end
```

2.
```
begin integer n; real recip;
    for n:=2 step 1 until 100 do
    begin recip:=1/n; print(recip, 1, 6); newline(1)
    end
end
```

3.
```
begin real ratio; integer count, jan, sales; jan:=read;
    print(100, 3, 3); newline(1);
    for count:=1 step 1 until 11 do
    begin sales:=read; ratio:=(sales/jan) * 100;
    print(ratio, 3, 3); newline(1);
    end
end
```

4.
```
begin integer n; real x, y, z;
for n:=1 step 1 until 10 do
begin x:=read; y:=read;
    z:=sqrt(y ↑ 2 + x ↑ 2); print(z, 3, 3)
    newline (1);
    end
end
```

5.
```
begin integer a; real r;
    for a:=1 step 1 until 100 do
        begin r:=sqrt(a/3.14); print(a, 3, 0); print(r, 3, 2);
        newline(1)
        end
end
```

12

6.

```
begin integer n, count1, count2; real p, term;
    p:=0; term:=1;
    for count1:=step 1 until 10 do
        begin for count2:=1 step 1 until 100 do
            begin term:=sign(term) * (1/n); p:=p+term;
                  term:=-term; n:=n+2;
            end;
        print(4 * p, 1, 8); newline(1)
        end
end
```

7.

```
begin integer n1, n2, n3;
    n1:=0; n2:=1;
    for n3:=n1+n2 while n3 < 10^8 do
        begin if n3 > 10^5 then
            begin print(n3, 10, 0); newline(1)
            end;
        n1:=n2; n2:=n3;
        end
end
```

Exercises 4.3
1.

```
begin array x[1: 10]; real average, devn, total, y, d; integer n;
    total:=0; for n:=1 step 1 until 10 do
        begin x[n]:=read; total:=total+x[n]
        end;
    average:=total/10; print(average, 3, 3); newline(1);
    devn:=0;
    for n:=1 step 1 until 10 do
        begin y:=abs(average-x[n]); if y > devn then
            begin devn:=y; d:=x[n]
            end
        end;
    print(d, 3, 3)
end
```

2.
```
begin array x[1: 5, 1: 3]; real big; integer m, n;
    big:=x[1, 1];
    for m:=1 step 1 until 5 do
    for n:=1 step 1 until 3 do if x[m, n]>big then big:=x[m, n];
    for m:=1 step 1 until 5 do
    for n:=1 step 1 until 3 do
    x[m, n]:=x[m, n]/big
end
```

3.
```
begin array y[1: 3, 1: 4]; real big; integer m, n, v, w;
    big:=y[1, 1]; m:=n:=1;
    for v:=1 step 1 until 3 do
    for w:=1 step 1 until 4 do if big<y[v, w] then
        begin big:=y[v, w]; m:=v; n:=w
        end;
    print(big, 3, 3); print(n, 1, 0); print(n, 1, 0)
end
```

4.
```
begin integer array p[1: 30]; integer i, j, k, m;
i:=1; p[1]:=3; j:=3;
L1: k:=0;
L2: k:=k+1; if p[k]>sqrt(j) then
    begin print(j, 2, 0); newline(1); p[i]:=j; i:=i+1;
    L3: j:=j+2; if j≠101 then goto L1 else goto L4
    end;
m:=j÷p[k]; if j = m * p[k] then goto L3 else goto L2;
L4: end
```

5.
```
begin integer m, n: integer array a [1: 38];
for m:=1 step 1 until 19 do
    begin a[m]:=m; a[m+19]:=m;
    end;
for n:=0 step 1 until 18 do
    begin for m:=1 step 1 until 19 do print(a[m+n], 2, 0);
    newline(1);
    end
end
```

Exercises 5.1

1.
```
      N = 1
   1  NSQ = N * N
      A = FLOATF(N)
      PRINT 2, N, NSQ, N * NSQ, SQRTF(A), A ** (1./3.)
   2  FORMAT(I4, 4X, I8, 4X, I10, 2(4X, F7.2))
      N = N+1
      IF (N − 101) 1, 3, 3
   3  STOP
      END
```

2.
```
      N = 2
   1  A = FLOATF(N)
      R = 1./A
      PRINT 2, R
   2  FORMAT(F9.6)
      N = N+1
      IF (N − 101) 1, 3, 3
   3  STOP
      END
```

3.
```
      N = 0
      READ 2, JAN
      I = JAN
   1  K = (I/JAN) * 100
   2  FORMAT(I4)
      PRINT 2, K
      N = N+1
      IF (N − 12) 4, 3, 3
   3  STOP
   4  READ 2, I
      GO TO 1
      END
```

4.

```
    N = 0
1   READ 2, X, Y
2   FORMAT(2F10.3)
    H = SQRTF(X ** 2 + Y ** 2)
    PRINT 3, H
3   FORMAT(F10.3)
    N = N + 1
    IF (N − 10) 1, 4, 4
4   STOP
    END
```

5.

```
    IA = 1
1   A = FLOATF(IA)
    R = SQRTF(A/3.14)
    PRINT 2, IA, R
2   FORMAT(I4, 8X, F6.2)
    IA = IA + 1
    IF (IA − 101) 1, 3, 3
3   STOP
    END
```

6.

```
    P = 0.
    K1 = 0
    K2 = 0
    A = 1.
    AN = 1.
1   T = A * (1./AN)
    P = P + T
    A = −A
    K2 = K2 + 1
    AN = AN + 2.
    IF (K2−100) 1, 2, 2
2   K2 = 0
    PRINT 3, P * 4.
3   FORMAT(F11.8)
    K1 = K1 + 1
    IF (K1−10) 1, 4, 4
4   STOP
    END
```

7.
```
        N1 = 0
        N2 = 1
     1  N3 = N2+N1
        N1 = N2
        N2 = N3
        IF (N3 − 10 ** 5) 1, 2, 2
     2  IF (N3 − 10 ** 8) 3, 4, 4
     3  PRINT 5, N3
     5  FORMAT(I10)
        GO TO 1
     4  STOP
        END
```

8.
```
        READ 1, A, B, D, P, Q, R
     1  FORMAT(6(F7.3, 3X))
        E = A * Q − B * P
        F = B * R − D * Q
        IF (E) 2, 3, 2
     2  X = F/E
        Y = (P * D − A * R)/E
        PRINT 4, X, Y
     4  FORMAT(2(F9.3, 8X))
        STOP
     3  IF (F) 7, 5, 7
     5  PRINT 6
     6  FORMAT(16H NOT INDEPENDENT)
        STOP
     7  PRINT 8
     8  FORMAT(14H INDETERMINATE)
        STOP
        END
```

Exercises 5.2

1.
```
        DO 1 N = 1, 100
        NSQ = N * N
        PRINT 2, N, NSQ, N * NSQ, SQRT(N), N ** (1./3.)
     2  FORMAT(I4, 4X, I8, 4X, I10, 2(4X, F7.2))
     1  CONTINUE
        STOP
        END
```

2.
```
      DO 1 N = 2, 100
         A = FLOATF(N)
         R = 1./A
         PRINT 2, R
2        FORMAT(F9.6)
1     CONTINUE
      STOP
      END
```

3.
```
      READ 2, JAN
2     FORMAT(I4)
      I = 100
      PRINT 2, I
      DO 1 N = 1, 11
      READ 2, K
      I = (K/JAN) * 100
1     PRINT 2, I
      STOP
      END
```

4.
```
      DO 1 N = 1, 10
      READ 2, X, Y
2     FORMAT(2F10.3)
      H = SQRTF(X ** 2 + Y ** 2)
      PRINT 3, H
3     FORMAT(F10.3)
1     CONTINUE
      STOP
      END
```

5.
```
      DO 1 IA = 1, 100
         A = FLOATF(IA)
         R = SQRTF(A/3.14)
      PRINT 2, IA, R
2     FORMAT(I4, 8X, F6.2)
1     CONTINUE
      STOP
      END
```

6.

```
                P = 0.
                A = 1.
                AN = 1.
        DO 1   K1 = 1, 10
        DO 2   K2 = 1, 100
                T = A*(1./AN)
                P = P + T
                A = -A
    2           AN = AN + 2
        PRINT 3, 4. * P
    3   FORMAT(F11.8)
    1   CONTINUE
        STOP
        END
```

Exercises 5.3

1.

```
        DIMENSION A(10)
            TOTAL = 0.
        READ 1, A
    1   FORMAT(10(F4.2, 2X))
        DO 2 N = 1, 10
    2   TOTAL = TOTAL + A(N)
            AVE = TOTAL/10.
            DEV = 0.
        DO 4   J = 1, 10
                Y = ABSF(AVE - A(J))
        IF (DEV - Y) 3, 4, 4
    3       DEV = Y
                D = A(J)
    4   CONTINUE
        PRINT 5, AVE, D
    5   FORMAT(2(F4.2, 10X))
        STOP
        END
```

2.

```
        DIMENSION X(5, 3)
                BIG = X(1, 1)
        DO 1       I = 1, 5
        DO 1       J = 1, 3
            IF(X(I, J) - BIG) 1, 1, 2
    2           BIG = X(I, J)
```

```
1   CONTINUE
    DO 3      I = 1, 5
    DO 3      J = 1, 3
          X(I, J) = X(I, J)/BIG
    STOP
    END
```

3.

```
    DIMENSION A (3, 4)
          BIG = A(1, 1)
          I = 1
          J = 1
    DO 1      K = 1, 3
    DO 1      L = 1, 4
IF    (A(K, L) – BIG) 1, 1, 2
2         BIG = A(K, L)
          I = K
          J = L
1   CONTINUE
    PRINT 3, BIG, I, J
3   FORMAT(F7.2, 2(6X, I2))
    STOP
    END
```

4.

```
DIMENSION IPRIME(30)
          I = 1
    IPRIME(1) = 3
          J = 3
1         K = 0
2         K = K + 1
          A = FLOATF(J)
          B = SQRTF(A)
          M = INTF(B)
    IF (IPRIME(K) – M) 4, 4, 3
3   PRINT 5, J
5   FORMAT(I3)
    IPRIME(I) = J
          I = I + 1
6         J = J + 2
    IF (J – 101) 1, 7, 7
7   STOP
4   M = J/IPRIME(K)
    IF(J – (M * IPRIME(K)) 2, 6, 2
    END
```

5.

```
DIMENSION N(38), J(19)
DO 1      M = 1, 19
          L = M + 19
          N(L) = M
1         N(M) = M
   DO 2      L = 0, 18
   DO 3      M = 1, 19
             K = M + L
3            J(M) = N(K)
             PRINT 4, J
4            FORMAT(19(I3, 2X))
2            CONTINUE
             STOP
             END
```

Exercises 6.1
1.

```
01   WEEKLY.
  02   NUMBER PICTURE 99999.
  02   FILLER PICTURE X(4).
  02   HOURS PICTURE 99.
  02   FILLER PICTURE X(8).
  02   OVERT PICTURE 99.
  02   FILLER PICTURE X(59).
```

2.

```
01   AMOUNT.
  02   SALES PICTURE 9999V99.
  02   MONTH PICTURE 99.
  02   CHANGES PICTURE S999.
  02   NAME PICTURE A(20).
  02   KIND PICTURE X(8).
  02   REPCODE PICTURE 999.
  02   AREA PICTURE XXXX.
```

3.

```
01   STOCK.
  02   PART PICTURE A(8).
  02   QUANTITY PICTURE 9(5).
  02   TYPE PICTURE 999.
  02   DESCPN PICTURE X(16).
  02   PRICE PICTURE 9999.
  02   FILLER PICTURE X(44).
```

4.

```
01  STOCK-RECORD.
    02  STOCKNO.
        03  TYPE PICTURE 999.
        03  UNIT PICTURE 999.
    02  DESCPN PICTURE X(20).
    02  BALANCE PICTURE 9999.
    02  RLEVEL PICTURE 9999.
    02  PURCODE
        03  AREA PICTURE 99.
        03  SUPPLIER PICTURE 99.
```

5.

```
01  PRINT-LINE.
    02  CODE PICTURE B(6)Z(5).
    02  NAME PICTURE B(4)A(20).
    02  AREA1 PICTURE B(6)ZZ.
    02  AREA2 PICTURE B(3)Z(3).
    02  NUMBER PICTURE B(4)Z(5).
    02  MONTH PICTURE BBBZZ.
    02  DAY PICTURE BBZZ.
    02  AMOUNT PICTURE B(4)££££.
```

Exercises 7.1

1.

```
Q1: PROCEDURE OPTIONS (MAIN);
DECLARE (N, NSQUARE) FIXED;
N = 1;
START: NSQUARE = N * N;
PUT LIST (N, NSQUARE, N * NSQUARE, SQRT(N),
    N **(1.0/3.0)) SKIP;
N = N + 1; IF N < 101 THEN GO TO START;
STOP; END;
```

2.

```
Q2: PROCEDURE OPTIONS (MAIN);
DECLARE N FIXED INITIAL (1); R FIXED (8 6);
START: R = 1.0/N; PUT LIST (R) SKIP;
N = N + 1; IF N < 101 THEN GO TO START;
STOP; END;
```

3.

```
Q3: PROCEDURE OPTIONS (MAIN);
DECLARE (JAN, SALES, N) FIXED,
RATIO FIXED (5, 2);
```

```
GET LIST (JAN); RATIO = 100.00;
PUT LIST (RATIO); N = 0;
START: GET LIST (SALES);
RATIO = 100 * (SALES/JAN);
PUT LIST (RATIO); N = N+1;
IF N < 11 THEN GO TO START;
STOP; END;
```

4.

```
Q4: PROCEDURE OPTIONS (MAIN);
DECLARE N FIXED, (X, H, Y) FIXED (6, 3);
N = 0;
START: GET LIST (X, Y);
H = SQRT(X ** 2 + Y ** 2);
PUT LIST (H); N = N+1;
IF N < 10 THEN GO TO START;
STOP; END;
```

5.

```
Q5: PROCEDURE OPTIONS (MAIN);
DECLARE A FIXED, R FIXED (6, 2);
A = 1;
START: R = SQRT(A/3.14); PUT LIST (A, R) SKIP;
A = A+1;
IF A < 101 THEN GO TO START;
STOP; END;
```

6.

```
Q6: PROCEDURE OPTIONS (MAIN);
DECLARE (A, K1, K2, N) FIXED, (P, T) FIXED (10, 8);
P = 0; A = 1; N = 1; K1 = 0; K2 = 0;
START: T = A * (1.0/N); P = P+T; A = -A; N = N+2;
K2 = K2+1; IF K2 < 100 THEN GO TO START;
K2 = 0; PUT LIST (4 * P); K1 = K1+1; IF K1 < 10 THEN
  GO TO START;
STOP; END;
```

7.

```
Q7: PROCEDURE OPTIONS (MAIN);
DECLARE (NA, NB, NC) FIXED; NA = 0; NB = 1;
COMMENCE: NC = NA+NB; NB = NC;
IF NC < 10 ** 5 THEN GO TO COMMENCE; IF NC < 10 ** 8
  THEN DO;
PUT LIST (NC) SKIP; GO TO COMMENCE; END;
STOP; END;
```

8.

```
Q8: PROCEDURE OPTIONS (MAIN);
DECLARE (A, B, D, P, Q, R, E, F, X, Y) FIXED (5, 2);
GET LIST (A, B, D, P, Q, R); E = A * Q - B * P;
  F = B * R - D * Q;
IF E > = 0 THEN GO TO LA; IF F > = 0 THEN GO TO LB;
PUT LIST ('NOT INDEPENDENT'); GO TO OUT;
LB: PUT LIST ('INDETERMINATE'); GO TO OUT;
LA: X = F/E; Y = (P * D - A * R)/E; PUT LIST (X, Y);
OUT: STOP; END;
```

Exercises 7.2

1.

```
Q1: PROCEDURE OPTIONS (MAIN);
DECLARE (N, NSQUARE) FIXED;
DO N = 1 TO 100;
NSQUARE = N * N; PUT LIST (N, NSQUARE,
  N * NSQUARE, SQRT(N), N **(1.0/3.0))
SKIP; END;
STOP; END;
```

2.

```
Q2: PROCEDURE OPTIONS (MAIN);
DECLARE N FIXED, R FIXED (8, 6);
DO N = 2 TO 100;
R = 1.0/N; PUT LIST(R) SKIP; END;
END;
```

3.

```
Q3: PROCEDURE OPTIONS (MAIN);
DECLARE (JAN, N, SALES) FIXED, RATIO FIXED (5, 2);
GET LIST (JAN); RATIO = 100.00;
PUT LIST (RATIO);
DO N = 1 TO 11;
GET LIST (SALES);
RATIO =100*(SALES/JAN);
PUT LIST (RATIO);
END;
STOP;
END;
```

4.

```
Q4: PROCEDURE OPTIONS (MAIN);
DECLARE N FIXED, (X, Y, H) FIXED (6, 3);
DO N = 1 TO 10;
GET LIST (X, Y);
H = SQRT(X ** 2 + Y ** 2); PUT LIST (H);
END;
STOP;
END;
```

5.

```
Q5: PROCEDURE OPTIONS (MAIN);
DECLARE A FIXED, R FIXED (6, 2);
DO A = 1 TO 100;
R = SQRT(A/3.14) PUT LIST (A, R) SKIP;
END;
STOP; END;
```

6.

```
Q6: PROCEDURE OPTIONS (MAIN);
DECLARE (A, K1, K2, N) FIXED, (P, T) FIXED (10, 8);
P = 0; A = 1; N = 1;
LA: DO K1 = 1 TO 10;
    LB: DO K2 = 1 TO 100;
    T = A * (1, 0/N); P = P + T; A = - A; N = N + 2;
    END LB;
PUT LIST (4 * P) SKIP;
END LA;
STOP; END;
```

Exercises 7.3

1.

```
Q1: PROCEDURE OPTIONS (MAIN);
DECLARE (TOTAL, Y, DEV, AVE) FIXED (9, 3), N(10)
    FIXED (9, 3), J FIXED (2);
TOTAL = 0;
LA: DO J = 1 TO 10;
    GET LIST (N(J)); TOTAL = TOTAL + N(J); END LA;
    AVE = TOTAL/10; DEV = ABS(N(1) - AVE); Y = N(1);
    LB: DO J = 2 TO 10;
    IF ABS(N(J) - AVE) > DEV THEN DO;
        DEV = ABS(N(J) - AVE); Y = N(J); END;
    END LB; PUT LIST (AVE, Y);
    STOP; END;
```

2.

```
Q2: PROCEDURE OPTIONS (MAIN);
BIG = MAX(A);
LA: DO I = 1 TO 5;
      LB: DO J = 1 TO 3; A(I, J) = A(I, J)/BIG;
END LA;
STOP; END;
```

3.

```
Q3: PROCEDURE OPTIONS (MAIN);
M = 1; N = 1; BIG = A(1, 1);
LA: DO V = 1 TO 3;
      LB: DO W = 1 TO 4;
      IF A(V, W) > BIG THEN DO;
            BIG = X(V, W); M = V; N = W; END;
END LA;
PUT LIST (BIG, M, N); STOP; END;
```

4.

```
Q4: PROCEDURE OPTIONS (MAIN);
DECLARE (PRIME(30), J, K, N, M) FIXED (3);
J = 1; PRIME(1) = 3; N = 3;
LA: K = 0;
LB: K = K+1;
IF PRIME(K) < = SQRT(N) THEN GO TO LK;
PUT EDIT (N) (F3, SKIP); PRIME(J) = N; J = J+1;
LD: N = N+2; IF N 101 THEN GO TO LA; GO TO OUT;
LK: M = N/PRIME(K); IF N = PRIME(K) * M THEN
    GO TO LD;
OUT: STOP; END;
```

5.

```
Q5: PROCEDURE OPTIONS (MAIN);
DECLARE (N(38), J(19), K, L, M) FIXED (2);
DO M = 1 TO 19;
L = M = 19; N(M) = M; N(L) = M;
END;
LA: DO L = 0 TO 18;
      LB: DO M = 1 TO 19;
            K = M+L; J(M) = N(K);
      END LB;
PUT LIST (J);
END LA;
STOP; END;
```

Exercises 8.1

1.

```
        MAIN 0
        CHAPTER 0
        N = 1
1)      PRINT(N) 3, 0
        PRINT(N * N)6, 0
        PRINT(N * N * N)10, 0
        PRINT(φSQRT(N))2, 4
        PRINT(φEXP(φLOG(N)/3))2, 4
        NEWLINE
        N = N + 1
        JUMP 1, N < 101
        END
        CLOSE
```

2.

```
        MAIN 0
        CHAPTER 0
        N = 1
        READ(F)
        A = 100
        PRINT(A)3, 3
1)      NEWLINE
        READ(E)
        A = 100 * (F/E)
        PRINT(A)3, 3
        N = N + 1
        JUMP L, N < 12
        END
        CLOSE
```

3.

```
        MAIN 12
        CHAPTER 0
        X → 9
        Y = 0
        N = 0
1)      READ(XN)
        X = Y + XN
        N = N + 1
        JUMP 1, N < 10
        A = Y/10
        PRINT(A)3, 3
        SPACE 8
```

```
      N = 0
      D = 0
3)    W = ϕMOD(A − XN)
      JUMP 2, D > W
      D = W
      V = XN
2)    N = N + 1
      JUMP 3, N < 9
      PRINT(V) 4, 3
      END
      CLOSE
```

4.

(assumes matrix stored in X0–X11)
```
      J = ϕMAX(X0, 0, 11)
      PRINT(XJ)3, 3
      NEWLINE
      JUMP 2, J = 0        |to avoid division into zero
      K = ϕINTPT(J/4)
      L = K + 1
      M = J − 4 * K + 1
1)    PRINT('ROW = ')
      PRINT(L)2, 0
      PRINT ('COLUMN=')
      PRINT(M)2, 0
      END
2)    L = 1
      M = 1
      JUMP 1
      CLOSE
```

5.

```
      MAIN 0
      CHAPTER 0
      π' = 0
      J = 1
      N = 1
      K = 1
2)    L = 1
1)    Y = 1.0/N
      X = J * Y
      π' = π' + X
      J = −J
      N = N + 2
      L = L + 1
```

13

```
        JUMP 1, L < 101
        PRINT(4 * π')1, 8
        NEWLINE
        K = K + 1
        JUMP 2, K < 11
        END
        CLOSE
```

6.

```
        MAIN 50
        CHAPTER 0
        W → 30
          I = 1
          WI = 3
          J = 3
    1)    K = 0
    2)    K = K + 1
          N = WK
          JUMP 5, N ⩽ φSQRT(J)
          PRINT(J) 3, 0
          NEWLINE
          WI = J
          I = I + 1
    3)    J = J + 2
          JUMP 1, J ≠ 101
          END
    5)    M = φINTPT(J/N)
          JUMP 3, J = M * N
          JUMP 2
          CLOSE
```

7.

```
        MAIN 0
        CHAPTER 0
        A = 1        indices would not hold 10⁸
        B = 1
    1)  D = B + A
        B = D
        A = B
        JUMP 1, D < &5
        JUMP 2, D > &8
        PRINT(D)10, 0
        NEWLINE
        JUMP 1
    2)  END
        CLOSE
```

8.

```
MAIN 0
CHAPTER 0
READ(A)
READ(B)
READ(C)
READ(D)
READ(E)
READ(F)
G = AE/BD
H = BF/CE
JUMP 1, G < & − 10
X = H/G
Y = (DC − AF)/G
PRINT(X)3, 3
SPACE 10
PRINT(Y)3, 3
END
1)  JUMP 2, ϕMOD((B/E) − (C/F)) < & − 10
    PRINT('INDETERMINATE')
    END
2)  PRINT('NOT INDEPENDENT')
    END
    CLOSE
```

Exercises 8.2

1.

```
MAIN 0
CHAPTER 0
N = 1(1)100
PRINT(N)3, 0
PRINT(N * N)6, 0
PRINT(N * N * N)10, 0
PRINT(ϕSQRT(N))2, 4
PRINT(ϕEXP(ϕLOG(N)/3))2, 4
NEWLINE
REPEAT
END
CLOSE
```

2.

```
MAIN 0
CHAPTER 0
READ(E)
    A = 100
```

```
PRINT(A)3, 3
N = 1(1)11
NEWLINE
READ(F)
A = 100 * (F/E)
PRINT(A)3, 3
REPEAT
END
CLOSE
```

3.

```
        MAIN 12
        CHAPTER 0
        X→9
        Y = 0
        N = 0(1)9
        READ(XN)
        Y = Y+XN
        REPEAT
        A = Y/10
        PRINT(A)3, 3
        SPACE 8
        D = 0
        W = φMOD(A−XN)
        JUMP 2, D>W
        V = XN
    2)  REPEAT
        PRINT(V)4, 3
        END
        CLOSE
```

4.

(Assumes matrix stored in X0–X11.)

```
        I = 1
        J = 1
        Y = X0
        N = 1(1)11
        JUMP 1, Y>XN
        Y = XN
        K = φINTPT(J/4)
        I = K+1
        J = N−4 * K+1
    1)  REPEAT
        PRINT(Y)3, 3
```

```
        PRINT(I)2, 0
        PRINT(J)2, 0
        END
```

5.

```
    MAIN 0
    CHAPTER 0
    π′ = 0
     J = 1
     N = 1
     K = 1(1)10
     L = 1(1)100
     Y = 1.0/N
     X = J * Y
    π′ = π′ + X
     J = −J
     N = N + 2
    REPEAT
    PRINT(4 * π′)1, 8
    NEWLINE
    REPEAT
    END
    CLOSE
```

6.

```
        MAIN 50
        CHAPTER 0
        W → 30
         I = 1
        WI = 3
         J = 3(2)99
         K = 0
    2)   K = K + 1
         N = WK
        JUMP 5, N ≤ φSQRT(J)
        PRINT(J)3, 0
        NEWLINE
        WI = J
         I = I + 1
    1)  REPEAT
        END
    5)  M = φINTPT(J/N)
        JUMP 1, J = M * N
        JUMP 2
        CLOSE
```

Exercises 8.3

1.

```
        MAIN 1009
        CHAPTER 0
        Y → 999
        A = 0
        I = 0
   1)   READ(YI)
        A = A + YI
        I = I + 1
   0)   READCH(M)
        JUMP 2, M = φCODE(*)
        JUMP 0, M ≠ φCODE(NL)    | spurious character—reads until
                                          newline
        JUMP 1
   2)   B = A/N
        PRINT('AVERAGE = ')
        PRINT(B)5, 3
        NEWLINE
        J = φMAX(Y0, 0, I − 1)
        PRINT('LARGEST = ')
        PRINT(YJ)8, 3
        NEWLINE
        K = φMIN(Y0, 0, I − 1)
        PRINT('SMALLEST = ')
        PRINT(YK)8, 3
        END
        CLOSE
```

2.

```
        MAIN 109
        CHAPTER 0
        M = 0
        N = 0
   1)   READ(A)
        JUMP 1, A > 0
        M = M + 1       | augment negative count
        JUMP 1
   0)   READCH(T)
        JUMP 2, T = φCODE(*)
        JUMP 1, T = φCODE(NL)
                N = N + 1            | erroneous character count
        JUMP 0
   2)   PRINT('NEGATIVE NUMBERS = ')
        PRINT(M)3, 0
```

```
NEWLINE
PRINT('ERRONEOUS CHARACTERS = ')
PRINT(N)4, 0
END
CLOSE
```

3.

```
    MAIN 0
    CHAPTER 0
     I = 0
     N = 1(1)10
     READ(K)
     JUMPDOWN 1
     I = I+K
     REPEAT
     K = I/10
     JUMPDOWN 1
     END
1)  PRINT(K * K)6, 0
     A = 1.0/K
     PRINT(A)1, 3
     NEWLINE
     RETURN
     CLOSE
     BK = R
3)     L = 0(1)3
     PRINT(BL)3, 0
     REPEAT
     NEWLINE
     RETURN
2)  K = K+1
     JUMP 3, R = 0        to avoid division into 0
     RETURN
     CLOSE
```

4.

```
    MAIN 130
    CHAPTER 0
    X → 125
    T = φCODE(1)          not a space for the start!
    N = 0                 word count
    P = 0                 packing position
1)  R = T                 previous character read
    READCH(T)
```

```
        PACK(X0, P, T)
        JUMP 2, T = φCODE(.)
            P = P + 1
        JUMP 1, T ≠ φCODE(SP)
        JUMP 1, R = T              | previous character a space
            N = N + 1              | word count augmented
        JUMP 1
     2) PRINT(N+1)3, 0
        PRINT('WORDS')
        END
        CLOSE
```

5.

```
        MAIN 520
        CHAPTER 0
        A → 511
         B = 0
        M = 1
        WIND TAPE(0, 1)
     1) N = 0
     2) READ(AN)
        N = N + 1
        JUMP 2, N < 512
        L = φMAX(A0, 0, 511)
        JUMP 4, B > AL
        B = AL
     4) WRITE(0, A0)
        M = M + 1
        JUMP 1
     0) READCH(P)
        JUMP 3, P = φCODE(*)
        JUMP 0, P ≠ φCODE(NL)     | faulty data found
        JUMP 2
     3) L = φMAX(A0, 0, N − 1)
        JUMP 5, B > AL
        B = AL
     5) PRINT('BLOCK')
        PRINT(M)4, 0
        PRINT('WORD')
        PRINT(N)3, 0
        SPACE 10
        PRINT('LARGEST = ')
        PRINT(B)7, 3
        END
        CLOSE
```

APPENDIX

BASIC

This appendix deals with Basic which differs from languages previously discussed as it is widely used for typing a program directly into a computer from a remote terminal, and so is less verbose than a more conventional batch-processing language. Other languages have been devised for this purpose but the majority are oriented towards a particular computer.

Basic, an acronym for Beginners All-purpose Symbolic Instruction Code, is a powerful yet simple language developed at Dartmouth College, New Hampshire, by Professors J. G. Kemeny and T. E. Kurtz and extended by General Electric (U.S.A.).

Compilers have been written for several computers and there are over 5000 users in Britain alone. Since Basic is oriented towards multi-access computer systems, it is especially useful for educational establishments, but it is equally appropriate for conventional batch processing. This appendix summarizes the essentials of Basic, which, although easy to master, is by no means jejune, since it includes instructions for character manipulation and matrix operations found in neither Algol nor Fortran. Compilation is speedy and provides an efficient object program.

The usual character set of Basic is the set of a terminal typewriter—the set for punched cards or paper tape can be found in the appropriate programming manual.

Store locations are referenced by variable names which consist of a letter or letters followed by a single digit such as L,J4,P0. Numerical constants may comprise up to nine digits and may contain a decimal point and minus sign. Acceptable constants could be 17, 5.21, $-.376$, .00317. Constants can also be written using E (denoting "times 10 to the power" (a similar Fortran facility is shown on page 57); e.g.

$$1.969E3 \quad = 1969$$
$$1234567E-2 = 12345.67$$
$$-376E-4 \quad = -.0376$$
$$2E-2 \quad \quad = .02$$

An alphanumeric constant can contain up to 15 characters (known as a string) in primes; e.g. "LORETTA" "EDWARD ELGAR". Values are assigned to variables by using a LET command; e.g.

```
100   LET A = 7
3500  LET J6 = .1056
```

Each command should be preceded by a line number, usually an integer between 1 and 99999. It is prudent to leave gaps when assigning line numbers so that additional commands may be inserted. A variable holding characters is followed by the symbol $; e.g.

```
1700  LET Q$ = "LORETTA IS FINE"
```

An arithmetic expression, which consists of variables and constants connected by the arithmetic operators $+$, $-$, $*$ (multiplication), $/$ and $\uparrow$ (exponentiation) is a more common form of the right-hand part of a LET command; e.g.

    1800   LET M = B$\uparrow$2 = 4*A*C

Arithmetic expressions are evaluated from left to right with the operators having similar priority to Algol (see p. 31). Brackets can be used to change the order of evaluation. Spaces on a line are ignored but a statement may not be longer than a line (usually 72 characters).

The power of the language is enhanced by the provision of mathematical functions. In the following list, X can be any arithmetic expression.

    SIN (X)

    COS (X)   X in radians

    TAN (X)

    ATN (X)   arctan (X)

    LOG (X)   natural log

    EXP (X) e^X

    ABS (X) $|X|$

    SQR (X) $\sqrt{X}$

    INT (X)   nearest integer $\leqslant X$

                     $INT(3.9) = 3$ $INT(-7.001) = -8$

A value may be inserted in several variables by a LET command; e.g.

    3900   LET A = B = J = K = X = $17.5 + LOG(P*(Q-R))$

The expression in the rightmost part is stored in A, B, J, K and X.

Commands are obeyed sequentially but if it is desired to depart from the normal sequence a GO TO command is used. GO TO 700 obeys the command on line 700 and then resumes obeying commands sequentially.

If it is desired to break the normal program sequence if a certain condition is true, an IF THEN command is used. In the following commands the program obeys command 2800 if $J < 8$.

    1200   IF J < 8 THEN 2800

    1300   LET A = J/N

               (several commands)

    2800   STOP

The form of the command is

    IF expression relational operator expression THEN line number

The relational operators are $=$, $>$, $<$, $> =$ (greater than or equal to), $< =$ (less than or equal to) and $< >$ (not equal to).

The numerical value of non-numeric characters can be ascertained from a programming manual. When strings of different lengths are compared, the shorter string and the corresponding part of the longer string are used.

Every program must usually terminate with an END statement. If it is desired to stop obeying commands at any point before this, a STOP command is used.

READ and DATA statements are used to read data into variables. The location of DATA statements in a program is arbitrary, provided that they are in the correct order, since all the data in such statements are assembled in a block before the program is executed. The READ command is of the form READ variable or variable list and the DATA statement of the form DATA data list. If a string in a DATA statement does not commence with a letter or if it contains commas, semicolons or spaces, it must be enclosed in primes. The following commands would insert 3 in X, 17.23 in Y, JULIA in L, .0326 in P, IT IS in R, − 5 in M and −.00003 in N.

```
3700   READ X, Y, L$
3800   LET A = 3.14
3900   DATA 3, 17.23
4000   LET K = 190435
4100   READ P, R$, M, N
4200   DATA JULIA, 3.26E − 2, "IT IS", − 5, − .3E − 4
```

If data are being inserted from a terminal typewriter during the execution of a program, an INPUT command is used. This causes a program halt whilst the appropriate data are typed. A typical INPUT statement could be

```
9400   INPUT X, Q$, T4
```

which would expect the typing of three items separated by commas.

The simplest PRINT statement is of the form PRINT sequence of expressions or single expression and prints up to five values per line on the terminal typewriter. Character strings can be printed separately or combined with numerical values; e.g.

```
7800   PRINT "VALUES ARE", T6, ABS(P + R/Z)
```

String variables may be intermixed with numerical variables. A print command without variables such as

```
1600   PRINT
```

will merely advance the paper 1 line. Details of more advanced print statements such as the use of TAB functions and image formats can be found in the appropriate programming manual.

The importance of loops in programming was stressed in Chapter 2. Basic FOR and NEXT statements provide an elegant means of loop control. The following sequence prints the square roots of 4, 7, 10 and 13.

```
3100   FOR L = 4 TO 13 STEP 3
3200 PRINT SQR (L)
3300 NEXT L
```

(L is known as the control variable). The FOR statement is of the form

FOR variable = expression TO expression STEP expression

If the step size is 1, STEP is omitted; e.g.

   4800 FOR E9 = 1 to 6

would give E9 the values 1, 2, 3, 4, 5, 6.

A GO TO or IF THEN statement must not enter commands between FOR and NEXT (thus bypassing the initialization of the control variable) unless there has been a previous jump out of the loop. If the initial, terminal or step values are expressions, these are evaluated once only at the start of the loop. Alteration of the control variable is permitted during the execution of the loop but is best avoided except by experienced programmers. After all the iterations have been performed, the control variable retains the value held during the final iteration. FOR loops may be nested.

The subscript of a subscripted variable is written in brackets after the variable name which must be a single letter. The subscript can be any integer expression greater than or equal to zero; e.g. A(0), E(9), L(K + M). If the value of a subscript is greater than 10, a dimension statement must be used to indicate the amount of store to be saved. The statement is of the form DIM singles (or repetitions of) variable name (number of elements); e.g.

   DIM X(70)   DIM I(15), K(20), L(3,4), R$(12)

It can be seen that up to two subscripts are allowed except for string variables (the array L defined above has three rows and four columns).

Some of the most original and useful Basic features are the matrix operation commands. These operate on matrices previously defined in a DIM statement and are

MAT READ X,Y,R	reads data row by row
MAT PRINT L,M,N,P	prints matrices in the usual form
MAT X = Y + E	adds two matrices
MAT A = B − U	subtracts two matrices
MAT G = H*K	multiplies two matrices
MAT N = (X + 7.1)*L	multiplies a matrix by a scalar expression in brackets
MAT L = INV(L)	inverts a matrix
MAT F = TRN(W)	transposes a matrix
MAT H = CON	sets all elements to 1
MAT V = ZER	sets all elements to 0
MAT R = IDN	sets diagonal elements to 1 and the rest to 0 yielding an identity matrix

The concept of subroutines was defined on page 17. A Basic subroutine is entered by a command of the form GOSUB line number. A RETURN command is used at any point in the subroutine where it is desired to return to the command after GOSUB. A GOSUB may be used inside a subroutine, but recursion (page 51) is illegal.

The following program reads eight numbers and prints the cube and square root of each number, their total and mean.

```
100   LET A = 0
200   DATA 41, 56, 19, 4, 1935, 17, 5, 1969
300   FOR D = 1 TO 8
400   READ B
500   LET A = A + B
600   GOSUB 1300
700   NEXT D
800   LET B = A
900   GOSUB 1300
1000  LET B = A/8
1100  GOSUB 1300
1200  STOP
1300  LET E = B↑(1.0/3.0)
1400  PRINT SQR(B),E
1500  RETURN
1600  END
```

In addition to the standard functions a programmer can in a single statement define his own functions by means of a DEF command. The name of such a function must contain three letters, the first two of which must be FN. A function is introduced by a line such as

```
8300   DEF FNL(X) = SQR(X↑3 + X↑4)
```

An invocation of the function in a program could be

```
9400   P = L + FNL(R)
```

The main features of Basic have now been discussed. Programming manuals contain details of other valuable features such as the creation and use of program and data files, the excellent edit and diagnostic facilities, a random-number generator and flexible print commands. Solutions are provided below to Exercises 5.3, problems 1–4 (page 80) in Basic.

1.
```
100   DATA (data list)
200   LET A = 0
300   READ B(K)
500   LET A = A + B(K)
600   NEXT K
700   LET E = A/10
800   LET D = 0
900   FOR L = 1 TO 10
1000  LF ABS(B(L) − E) > D THEN 1400
1100  NEXT L
1200  PRINT E,F
1300  STOP
1400  LET D = ABS(B(L) − E)
1450  LET F = B(L)
1500  GO TO 1100
1600  END
```

2.

```
400   LET B = X(1,1)
500   FOR I = 1 TO 5
600   FOR J = 1 TO 3
700   IF X(I,J) > B THEN 1200
800   NEXT J
900   NEXT I
1000  MAT X = (1.0/B)*X
1001  MATPRINT X
1100  STOP
1200  LET B = X(I,J)
1300  GO TO 800
1400  END
```

3.

```
400   LET B = X(1,1)
500   LET I = J = 1
600   FOR K = 1 TO 4
700   FOR L = 1 TO 3
800   IF X(K,L) > B THEN 1300
900   NEXT L
1000  NEXT K
1100  PRINT B,I,J
1200  STOP
1300  LET I = K
1400  LET J = L
1500  LET B = X(K,L)
1600  GO TO 900
1700  END
```

4.

```
100   DIM P(50)
150   LET I = 1
200   LET J = P(1) = 3
300   LET K = 0
400   LET K = K+1
500   IF P(K) < = INT(SQR(J)) THEN 1200
600   PRINT J
700   LET P(I) = J
800   LET I = I+1
900   LET J = J+2
1000  IF J < 100 THEN 300
1100  STOP
1200  LET M = INT(J/P(K))
1300  IF J = P(K)*M THEN 900
1400  GO TO 400
1500  END
```

INDEX